Concepts of Operational Research

By
PATRICK RIVETT

LONDON
C. A. WATTS & CO. LTD.
1968

First published 1968

SBN 296 34706 X

Printed in Great Britain by Alden & Mowbray Ltd
at the Alden Press, Oxford

36/622

THE NEW THINKER'S LIBRARY

General Editor: RAYMOND WILLIAMS

Concepts of Operational Research

TO ANN

PREFACE

AT a time when so many of my friends and colleagues are producing books on the problems of decision making, it might be wise to show why I am adding yet another to the list. During the period of the development of the fields of study which are outlined in this book, both layman and scientist alike have become conscious of the increasing gulf which seems to separate them. The cause of this lies equally in differences of attitude and differences of language.

This book is an attempt to bridge the gulf. It tries to outline the reasons for the approach which the scientist takes to decision-making problems and why we do not accept that intuition and experience are the best, or even valid, guides. Inevitably jargon words will creep in. For this I make no apology. It would be impossible to describe cricket to a foreigner without using words such as wicket, boundary, over. If we want to understand another area of study, we have to master the elements of the language, but I hope the jargon is kept to a minimum.

All my friends in operational research will agree that this is not a book for the O.R. specialist. Any attempt to describe the subject so briefly must be superficial. My friends will also discern the extent of my debt to them all. I have received most helpful comments on portions of the book from R. T. Eddison and G. Thomas, and the influence of both these and many others, including Professor Russell Ackoff, Stafford Beer, R. W. Shephard, Professor K. D. Tocher, is plain to see. Such good qualities as the book has are theirs. The faults and imperfections are all my own.

I would like to express my gratitude to Miss D. Underwood and Miss J. Armer who typed out the manuscript so many times.

B. H. P. R.

CONTENTS

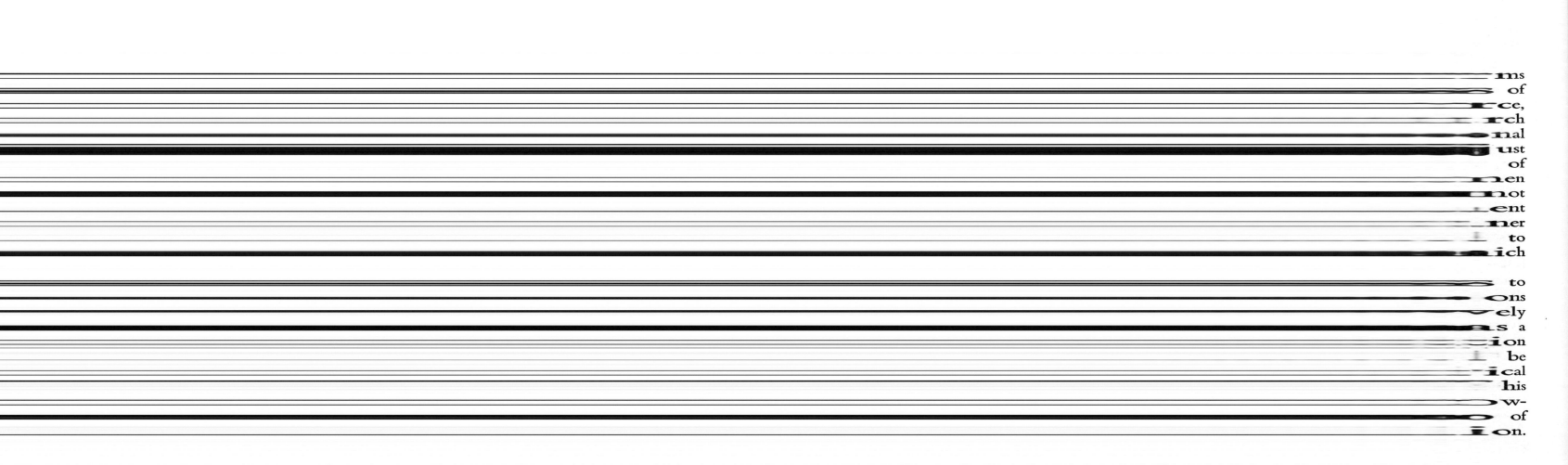

It may be a di

but arithmetic

the research sc

problems of th

There is ho

lems which d

that this range

increasing com

As is well

industries in B

operated in a s

garage. These

the same man

his business, he

ties of his prod

probably only

revolution can

ment and mach

ing equipment

away from the

been in bonda

of raw materia

been imposed

moved. In addi

the capital equ

was such as ma

dual company

ment of the sin

in the size of th

no longer man

nings of the sp

crude breakdo

tion, marketing

As time went

I

ON THE EVOLUTION OF
AN ATTITUDE

The purpose of this book is to outline in non-technical terms
the way in which natural scientists study the consequences of
decisions in complex situations not only in business, commerce,
and government, but also in the military field. The research
work in this general area has come to be called operational
research and stems from pioneer studies carried out just
before the Second World War by groups of scientists of
various disciplines who attempted to study the use of men
and weapons systems within a context of conflict. It is not
the purpose of this book to review the historical development
of operational research, but rather to try to expose the manner
in which these scientists approached their problems and to
show why this is an important field of activity, one with which
the general reader should make acquaintance.

Why should decision making be so complex a study as to
warrant scientific research? There are indeed many situations
in which the problem facing the decision maker is relatively
simple. He is completely aware of his objective. He has a
limited range of action and for each possible course of action
it is possible for him to predict with certainty what will be
the consequence, and to translate this into a single numerical
form appropriate to use as a measure of the attainment of his
objective. In these situations he has limited choice, full knowledge of consequence, full knowledge of the relationship of
consequence to his objective. Hence he is in a trivial situation.

It may be a difficult one for him to control as an executive, but arithmetically and structurally the system is trivial and the research scientist is not concerned with decision-making problems of this nature or type.

There is however a wide range of decision-making problems which do not fall into this category. We can observe that this range is constantly growing and is a reflection of the increasing complexity of industry and government in general.

As is well known, until the industrial revolution most industries in Britain employed only a handful of workers and operated in a space which would now be filled by a two-car garage. These small companies were owned and managed by the same man. This one man was quite competent to develop his business, he knew all his employees, he knew the capabilities of his product and he was fully in touch with the market, probably only local, which he served. With the industrial revolution came the introduction of power-generating equipment and machine tools. The development of power-generating equipment meant that these small businesses could move away from the sources of natural power to which they had been in bondage and move closer to the sources of labour and of raw material. Hence the limit on increase of size which had been imposed by restriction of labour availability was removed. In addition, increase in size became necessary, because the capital equipment involved in the industrial revolution was such as markedly to increase the viable size of the individual company. The need for extra capital led to the replacement of the single owner by a group of creditors. The increase in the size of the business meant that the single manager could no longer manage the whole business. This led to the beginnings of the specialization of the management task. The first crude breakdown of the single manager's task was to production, marketing, raw material buying, personnel and finance. As time went on, men responsible for these fields were faced with the need to subdivide their specialities yet again. This was the beginning of the very complex management structure with which we are familiar today. As companies continued to grow and build separate plants in new locations, the complex of managers had to be replicated. The large modern company has a structure, therefore, which is the result of an evolutionary process and which reflects the difficulty of control from the centre.

Hence we have seen growth through delegation, and it is, in passing, interesting to query the extent to which such delegation will continue when the central parts of organizations have the ability, through large-scale data processing, to control far more than they have been accustomed to.

In parallel with this growth of industry went a similar explosive growth of science itself. We are painfully conscious of the rate of this growth today. Not only are ninety per cent of the graduate scientists the world has ever produced, still alive (officially at least), but in a field such as chemistry half the papers and books on the subject ever published were published in the last ten years. The early growth of the sciences which are relevant to the management process was more leisurely. At the time of the industrial revolution groups of physicists became more interested in the application of available knowledge to machine processes, rather than in the derivation of new knowledge. Hence mechanical engineering was created, like Eve, out of a rib of physics. These engineers initially concerned themselves with increasing the productivity of machine processes. At the turn of the century it became clear that further increases of productivity would only be gained if attention were devoted to the interaction of man and machine. In this way attempts to measure human work were made and from these came the development of method study and industrial engineering. Mechanical engineers and chemists together studied the relationship between product, process, and machine and as a result chemical engineering came into importance as a subject which had relevance to the industrial situation.

It is often thought that the interaction of man and machine in the industrial revolution led to the first attempts at work measurement and that Taylor's famous studies, in the 1890s at the Bethlehem Steel Company, of the effort involved in shovelling were absolutely original. However the evolution of what is called the science of shovelling myth has been exploded,[1] and studies of work measurement in shovelling are traced back through W. S. Jevons (1883), Charles Babbage (1851), Charles Coulomb (1781), De la Hire (1699) and (almost inevitably!) to Leonardo da Vinci.

Further importance was given to the study of man himself and this led to the development of psychology, sociology and industrial relations. During the early years of this century it was realized that further information and data were needed about the activity of the State itself and hence statistics came into importance, first of all as a data-collecting mechanism. Statistics grew in importance particularly in the economic field. The reaction between statistician and mathematician led to the development of probability and mathematical statistics through studies of variability of machine performance and of the characteristics of sampling inspection schemes.

Economics has already been mentioned. The use of the scientific method, both in studies of the firm, micro-economics, and in the study of the State, macro-economics, is well known and has been well documented. Under the influence of the higher levels of taxation after the First World War, accounting gradually became more important, first as a way of checking on the revenue which the individual and the corporation had to yield to the State, and then, as a natural

---

[1] COOPER, W. W., LEAVITT, H. J. and SHELLY, M. W., *New Perspectives in Organization Research*, (Wiley).

extension, in the control of financial matters within the industrial organization.

And so we see in parallel the fragmentation of the management task stemming from the single owner-manager and the fragmentation of the technological sciences stemming from physics. But in all of this development there is one curious and conspicuous gap. This was caused by the failure of the scientist to observe that the result of the increase in complexity of industrial processes and of industrial products has been to lay on the desk of the manager a much more difficult kind of problem for his decision.

It was a particular kind of technological research which was being carried out before the last World War which led to the recognition that the scientist had something of value to say about the consequences of decisions. At that time groups of physical scientists had been studying the interference of radio reception by low-flying aircraft. It was found that this was due to the reflection of radio waves from the aircraft and this led to the applied research which culminated in the development of radar. When these radar research scientists had the task of introducing the radar sets to Army units, they found themselves doing something much beyond this straight technological task. They were asking questions about the effective use of radar in the field compared with the way it reacted in the laboratory under trial conditions. They found that radar was temperamental, its performance was affected by ground configuration and by local considerations. It was clearly seen that there was but little use in obtaining rapid knowledge that an aircraft was in the sky a hundred miles away, if this knowledge was not translated into effective action by ground and airborne defence forces. Hence numbers of trials of the use of operations rooms and the control and command system generally were carried out. These radar research scientists therefore were studying the *operational* use of radar. They

began to be called radar operational research teams to distinguish them from the radar research teams from which
they had stemmed. In time the use of the word radar was
dropped from the phrase and their subject began to be called
operational research. Every time we use the phrase operational
research we are acknowledging the military beginnings of the
subject, rooted in the development of radar.

By the beginning of the Second World War these operational research teams had carried out many studies of the
operational use of radar by ground and air defence forces.
When war broke out, the other services, the Army and the
Navy, began to employ scientists for studying the use of men
and weapons systems under battle conditions. These were the
first attempts by scientists to structure and to measure a battle
problem in the same way as they would structure and measure
problems of physics, chemistry or biology. It was found that,
once they were able to understand the technology of the
systems they were studying, they could make significant
improvements to the way in which these systems were controlled. There is in most sciences a classical study which
somehow brings together the essence of the idea in a vivid
way. Operational research also has one such study associated
with it.[1]

During the war years, after the fall of France, the Germans
mounted a submarine offensive on the Atlantic convoys
coming to Britain. This offensive was mounted from the
Bay of Biscay ports and the submarines would normally travel
on the surface to and from the battle-grounds. From south-
west England, Coastal Command operated a screen of aircraft loaded with depth charges. The task of these aircraft was
to seek out the submarines and, when there was a sighting,
a ritual operation took place. The aircraft would manœuvre
into position for bombing, fly in, and drop its depth charges

[1] *Operational Research in the R.A.F.* (H.M.S.O.).

around the site of the submarine. At the same time the submarine having heard or seen the aircraft would crash dive. The one constant feature in the operation was that the depth charges were pre-set to go off at the depth at which they had their maximum physical effect. As can be imagined, there is a minimum depth above which depth charges will not fire because the arming pistol which operates on impact with the water has a natural delay associated with it. At a shallow depth some of the energy of the depth charge will be expended in throwing water into the sky. At great depths the pressure of water will muffle the explosion. Somewhere in between there will be an optimum point at which the depth charges have their greatest killing radius. This was one hundred feet.

Unfortunately a feature of the whole operation was the relatively low rate of sinkings of submarines. The operational research team of Coastal Command was invited to study the operation with a view to making recommendations for improving this rate. Now in this situation there are obvious technological and logistic factors which can yield improvement. More aircraft could be put on patrol. The bomb-sight could be improved. More powerful depth charges could be developed. The sighting probabilities could be increased by improving the airborne radar which enabled submarines to be detected. All these are technological approaches and all of them would yield an improvement. It was not the task of the team to reach for the pie in the sky. It was their task to take the equipment which was available and to show how it could be used to a better advantage.

One feature of all case studies is that when they are presented, they are presented in a nutshell and the reader may wonder what the research team did in the second week of the investigation. The team first of all spent some time flying with aircraft on patrol and observing what went on. They then analysed pilots' logs and built up a picture of the whole operation. From this they tried to see what features were present in operations which resulted in a sinking, compared with features which were not present in operations which resulted in failure (from the point of view of the attacking aircraft).

Analyses were made of the effect of the height of the aircraft, its course and its speed, the position of the submarine when sighted, its course and its speed. None of these features yielded success. Eventually however, someone asked the simple question, where was the submarine when the depth charge went off? It is when the depth charge explodes that the moment of truth occurs and the whole operation is geared to lead up to this moment. Hence the flight logs were examined, not from the point of view of the starting of the operations in the aircraft, but simply in terms of the very localized question of where the submarine was when the depth charge went off. Now the depth of the submarine can be deduced in terms of the time it has been submerged at the moment the depth charge explodes. An analysis of the data showed that in nearly all the cases the submarine was still on the surface or within twenty feet of it. Very rarely had the submarine been submerged long enough to take itself down to within the killing radius of the depth charge, one hundred feet.

Now there is another feature which has to be contended with in this operation. Submarines which are nearer the surface are also more densely packed than those which have been submerged longer which will have spread out over a wider zone. Figs. 1 and 2 show these features.

In addition the killing radius of the depth charge increases with depth of setting up to 100 ft, and these two factors together show the probability of sinking a submarine in terms of the setting of the depth charge (Figs. 3 and 4).

It was not very difficult for the team to suggest that the setting of depth charges be reduced, but for many reasons

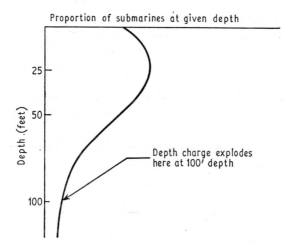

Fig. 1. Vertical distribution of submarines at time of explosion of depth charge

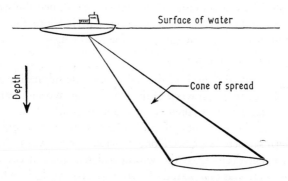

Fig. 2. Spatial distribution of submarines as they dive

this was resisted. This argument went higher and higher in the reaches of the war effort and finally arrived at the Cabinet table. The story (perhaps apocryphal) goes that the War Cabinet decided that there would be one trial week at the old setting and one trial week at the new setting. The operational research team were asked to estimate the improvement in the rate of sinkings if the setting was reduced to thirty feet.

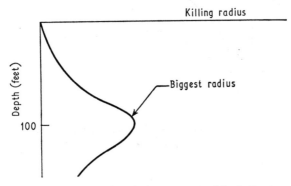

Fig. 3. Killing rates of depth charge in terms of depth of setting

Their calculations suggested a doubling of this sinking rate and the trial was mounted. Now when one studied the week by week sinkings of submarines over a period into the past the numbers went something like the following—

0 0 1 0 1 2 0 0 1 1 0 1 0 0 0 1

In the first trial week of the old setting one submarine was sunk. In the first trial week of the new setting two submarines were sunk. This was taken as a triumphant justification of the whole of the processes of probability mathematics and of modern science. A glance along previous weeks would have shown that even when the setting had remained at the old figure there was one period of two successive weeks in which the sinkings were one in one week and two in the following week. However in operational research, as in other sciences, one learns to accept luck when it comes and so the change to the new setting was made. In the long run there was such an increase in the sinkings of submarines, that the German radio claimed that the British had developed a new secret weapon for anti-submarine warfare. All that had been done was to use what was to hand more intelligently.

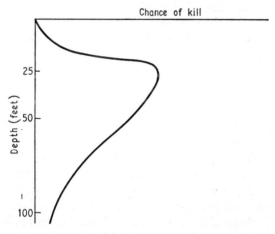

Fig. 4. Chance of killing submarine in terms of depth of setting

Now the reason for introducing this example, and the reason why it has become such a classic, is that it shows the elements of the operational research approach. It can be noted that the objective of the study was set as "to increase the sinkings of submarines". Now this is not the real objective. The objective was not just to kill Germans and sink submarines in the Bay of Biscay. It was to get the convoys through and a question which had to be asked in parallel with this study was whether the effort deployed on attacking submarines was worth while or whether it should have been replaced by more localized effort in protecting convoys. However, accepting the description of the objective of the study we notice the following stages—

1. The observation of the operation
2. Understanding the technology of the operation
3. The collection of basic quantitative data
4. Sorting and analysis of data
5. Derivation of a hypothesis
6. Decision for change
7. Forecasting the results of change in a quantitative manner
8. Careful implementation and the check on the validity of the hypothesis.

We notice, in the example, the way in which the hypothesis was presented. It was presented as a way of showing what is likely to happen if different courses of action are undertaken, that is what proportion of submarines will be sunk in terms of the setting of the depth charge. The important thing to notice is that it was not necessary to carry out trials at all the different possible depths of setting and estimate from these trials the shape of the curve in Fig. 4 above. The only information available was the rate of sinkings at one hundred feet. To this was added a knowledge of the characteristics of submarines and of depth charges. This is what is meant by understanding the technology and the structure of the problem. From all this, it was possible to deduce a wide range of different results of different courses of action which might be taken.

This quantitative statement of the consequences of the different controllable decisions of a decision maker, is called the *model*. The model is central to operational research as it is to all science. Science is rich in model building. Newton's model of the universe united, in a few statements of algebra, the movement of the planets in the furthest heavens to the collision of billiard balls on a billiard table. Keynes's model of the economy forecasts the effect of different levels of savings and investment on the health of the economy as a whole. An engineer builds a force diagram of the forces in the structure of a bridge and consequently does not need to experiment by building bridges and seeing how many of them stand up. The model to the engineer is very much like the model to the operational research worker. The engineer can only experiment in limited fashion. When he gets to his grand design he has to be sure that the thing will work. His model, the force diagram, consists basically of straight lines drawn on a piece of paper. In the real structure of the bridge the forces are transmitted by millions of molecules acting and reacting on each other. The engineer's model is a many–one transform in which the many factors in the real-life situation are represented by one factor in his model. It is a simplification which works, because what has been omitted is not important and what is retained is. There is, therefore, a large subjective element in model building and the operational research worker at the stage of the construction of his model is an artist rather than a scientist. In the next chapter we shall try to show something of the principles of model building.

II

THE METHODOLOGY OF
MODEL BUILDING

As has been said, model building is central to operational research as it is central to any science. The importance of model building will vary in different sciences, and will in general be related to the difficulty, whether financial or physical, of experimentation. In operational research we are in a situation in which experimentation is not as impossible as in astronomy, and not as expensive as in physics. But it is still a difficult subject in which to carry out real-life experiments. This means that the central craft of operational research is the craft of understanding a decision situation and of building the structure of it. Let us give an example of how not to construct a model. This example will illustrate the perils of statistical method unreasoningly applied.

Some years ago the author was working in the National Coal Board and the research team at that time was studying the factors affecting the comparative economics of diesel and battery locomotives in use underground. The object of the study was to find circumstances in which one locomotive was likely to be cheaper in use than the other, as this would affect the whole development programme of the Board which was then getting under way. The team visited all the diesel and battery locomotive installations in use in Britain and from these collected complete cost data. These data were analysed to try to show the overall relationship between certain crude factors and the costs, week by week, of the particular system.

They were analysed according to the total length that coal was hauled, the tonnage handled per shift, the gradient, the total ton mileage and so on. Statistical tests of all these factors against the weekly costs showed no relationships. After spending a great deal of time on these analyses the statisticians in the team became more and more depressed.

It was then that the engineers in the team took over from the statisticians. They pointed out that if life is to have any meaning then the laws of physics and of engineering would apply to locomotives in use underground just as they would elsewhere. Consequently the energy costs of each of the systems studied must be related to the work done by the locomotive. So, in each of the systems visited, the energy cost for the diesel or the battery locomotive was extracted and related in average terms to the work done by the locomotive in each shift. It was then formulated that the cost of maintaining the track would be related to the total length of track. The depreciation cost of the locomotive would be related to its size and so the depreciation cost of the locomotive was expressed as so much per peak hauling need. In this way all the costs of the system were broken down into groups and the groups were expressed in terms of what appeared, from physical knowledge, to be the relevant unit. This gave a method of synthesizing the costs of a hypothetical installation. It also showed the way in which installations could be checked to see in which particular respects they were cheaper or more expensive than should be expected by this group costs approach.

This is what is meant by looking at the structure of a problem. The approach of the bad statistician is to assume that because he knows nothing about the real-life situation, nobody else knows anything about it either. It is when we ignore structure and merely try to get statistical associations that we can get the nonsense correlations that are so beloved of statisticians. We know, for example, that if we plot in a graph on the horizontal scale, as shown in Fig. 5, the immigration of storks into Norway year by year and on the vertical scale the birth rate in Norway year by year, we will get a very close relationship.

The relationship is so good that one is tempted to use a stork gun as a method of birth control. A reason for the

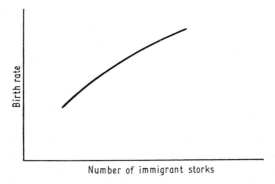

Fig. 5. *Apparent relationship between immigration of storks into Norway and the Norwegian birth rate*

relationship, however, is that in agricultural communities, in times of good harvest there is prosperity and with prosperity the birth rate may go up. Also in times of good harvest there is an abundance of grain and abundance of grain means more of all forms of wild life, including storks.

In a similar fashion one can see an apparent relationship (Fig. 6) between the membership of the Conservative Party in each of the counties of England and the drunkenness rate. The reason for this is that in more densely populated areas there will be more Conservatives, and indeed Methodist ministers and lamp-posts as well. Where there is a densely populated area the drunkenness rate will go up as this is a feature of urban life. Hence drunkenness rates will be related to Conservatives, Methodist ministers and lamp-posts also. But you cannot reduce them by converting Conservatives to socialism, Methodists to Papistry or by uprooting lamp-posts, since the connexion is not a direct cause and effect.

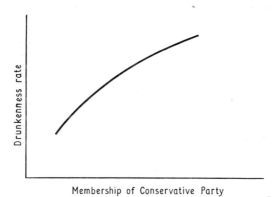

Fig. 6. Apparent relationship between numbers of Conservative Party in the counties of England and the local drunkenness rate

Let us give one final cautionary tale. If the reader is shown the following series and asked to predict the next member, what would be his choice—

1,860   1,880   1,900   1,920   1,940   1,960   ?

Surely 1,980.

But, if we are now told (as is true) that in these years, the man who was elected President of the United States died in office, and that no President in the last hundred years has died in office who did not win the election in one of these years, would we still forecast 1980? Our knowledge of the background of the data changes our forecast.

Our forecast is changed in terms of the significance we

attach to the series of numbers. If nothing else is known, then 1980 is a reasonable forecast.

In the light of the additional information, however, 1980 is unreasonable—given that the series only has six terms in it. But, suppose the series went back with complete regularity for two hundred instead of one hundred years? Then, if one was offered the nomination in 1980 would one not be tempted to reply, "I don't know what is going on, but thank you very much, I'd rather not"? Every statistical test has to be related to all our other knowledge, it must not be treated as separate from the fabric of human experience.

These simple examples show very clearly the need to inquire at the beginning of a study into the structure of the problem. The following example will illustrate this. Some years ago the operational research group at the Case Institute of Technology in the United States was invited by a large oil company to carry out a study of the factors influencing the sale of petrol from petrol stations. When Russell Ackoff and his small team arrived at the oil company they found that two previous studies had been attempted in this area. One had been carried out by motivational research psychologists who had undertaken depth interviews of motorists and had built up a picture of their relationship with the petrol stations they used. The only useful feature which seemed to come from this study, however, was the dominance of the petrol station attendant as a father figure. The second approach to which the oil company then turned was the building of an economic model of this situation. Groups of economists were asked to analyse the situation and they listed for each petrol station up to twenty-five factors which could be taken as influencing the situation. Large-scale statistical analyses were carried out in which the sales of petrol related by equations of the following kind—

$$\text{Sales} = a_1 x_1 + a_2 x_2 + \ldots + a_{25} x_{25} + a_{26} x_1 x_2 + \ldots$$

As can be seen this is not a simple relationship and large-scale regression analyses were carried out to estimate the factors a_1, a_2, etc.

However, as a result of these analyses only half the variability in petrol sales could be accounted for and it was apparent that this study was not leading to success. When Ackoff's team arrived the economists explained what they were trying to do. An engineer in the team got more and more irate. Eventually he could contain himself no longer. Good Heavens (or the American equivalent of it) he said, we can express the whole of the complexity of modern physics

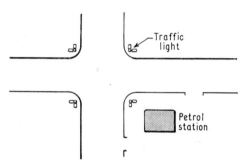

Fig. 7. Location of petrol station at cross-roads

in one simple equation $E = mc^2$. What is so special about selling petrol to motorists from petrol stations that it needs equations with at least thirty terms? What has been neglected, he said, is that the numbers in the equations represent things which are happening on the ground. Why not go out and look at the structure of this problem?

Now the petrol stations concerned were in urban areas and hence were in the usual grid pattern of American towns. The folklore of the oil industry was to locate petrol stations at corners and so the situation was as shown in Fig. 7.

All the cars which enter the petrol station will certainly both enter and leave the road junction. How many ways are there in and out of the junction?

Consider cars which approach up the road from the south. Some of them will go straight through to the north, others will turn east, others west, while the occasional woman driver will do a U-turn in the middle of the road and go out again southwards. Hence for cars entering from the south there are four possible routes, and with four roads, there are sixteen possible ways in and out of the road junction.

The team sat at petrol stations and logged vehicles, according to their route into the junction and their route out of it. They built up a pattern which showed the proportion of cars on each of the sixteen routes which used the petrol station (Fig. 7). They found, to their surprise, that ninety-five per cent of the sales of petrol at the station were accounted for by only three out of the sixteen routes, and the same three every time. Referring to Fig. 7, the three routes were (1) cars entering from south and leaving through north, (2) cars entering from south and leaving through east, (3) cars coming in from the east and leaving to the south. These three routes cradled the petrol station in question and gave possibilities of avoiding a red traffic light at the road junction. From these results, estimates could be made, in terms of traffic density at any road junction, of the potential sales of petrol from a petrol station located there. But something more important emerged. There was another part of the folklore of the American oil industry, that if there was already a petrol station at a site then it was not worth buying another one at the same cross-roads. But when one looks at the three routes which give the ninety-five per cent of the sales on the south-eastern location, one can see that none of these routes would give a contribution to the similar percentage for a petrol station at any of the other three locations. Consequently it was worth while building stations at cross-roads because there would be ninety-five per cent of sales at least still there, and, also, because the other oil companies thought the sites were not worth having they could be bought cheaply.

From this can be seen, in an admirable way, what is meant by the structure of a problem. The structure of the problem here is that there are things moving along four channels and we have to look at the probabilities that these things in movement will go into a certain off-shoot area. This is what is missed out in the economic model building and in the motivational research approach.

Some models can occasionally be fabricated in a physical form. For example, suppose we want to build a factory to supply a demand for a product of twenty tons a day in Cardiff, thirty tons a day in Manchester, and fifty tons a day in London. Given that transport costs are proportional to the product of tonnage and distance carried, where should the factory be located so as to minimize delivery costs? It is possible to work this out mathematically, but by a curious chance the solution can be derived physically in the following way.

Take a cut-out map of England and pass a piece of string through a smooth hole at each of Cardiff, Manchester and London. Under the map, at the end of each string, fasten a weight proportional to the tonnage to be delivered at the destination through which the string passes: in the present example, two ballbearings under Cardiff, three under Manchester and five under London. Join the three pieces of string together in a knot on top of the map and allow the weights to pull the knot to an equilibrium position. The point where the knot comes to rest is the minimum transport position. This approach will work for any number of destinations and tonnages but breaks down if the costs of transport are not proportional to ton mileage. The physical model also breaks down if we are trying to locate optimally more than one factory.

The physical model shows up an interesting fallacy. It is intuitively obvious (and quite wrong) to select as the minimum position the centre of gravity of weights of 20, 30 and 50 placed at Cardiff, Manchester, and London, for the centre of gravity is not necessarily the equilibrium position. In the special case of three destinations lying on a straight line the optimum location is at B no matter where B is, between A and C.

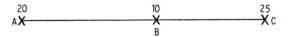

Fig. 8. Points of demand on a straight line with the amounts demanded

If the knot is to the right of B, there will be a force of 30 to the left and 25 to the right and so the knot will move leftwards: similarly for a knot to the left of B. Although the centre of gravity will also change according to the position of B, it will only be at B itself when $\dfrac{AB}{BC} = \dfrac{25}{20}$. Another curious by-product is that if we now introduce a fourth destination, D, on the straight line, as long as its requirement is less than 5, the optimum location is still at B, *no matter* how far away D be placed.

The familiar problem of stock control provides another example of the way in which models are built. Let us consider the following: we have a production process which makes irregular demands for an item; we also know that when we make a demand for this item from the suppliers there will be a time-lag until the supply is received; consequently we are faced with two sources of variability, a variable demand and a variable supply. In order to link these two and to protect the demand from variations in the supply we operate a stock of the items.

This stock is essentially a link in a chain and as a link it buffers the variable demand from the variable supply. How should we create a model of the decision: how often should we order and how much?

We have to ask certain questions about the situation itself. First of all what is the pattern of demand? If we analyse this we will find that it is irregular, in that different numbers of items are demanded each day. Sometimes only a few, at other times many. But if we analyse the day by day demands over, say, one hundred days and plot them on a graph we will find they vary according to a pattern as shown in Fig. 9.

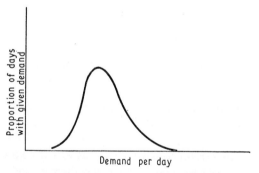

Fig. 9. Statistical distribution of the demand per day

This gives a picture of the demand which might be made on the stockholding point day by day and we would further test that the demand in any one day is independent of the demand on the previous day.

We now ask the same question about the supply. An analysis over past history, say over one hundred orders, will show that sometimes when a request for more items is made the demand is met very quickly whereas on other occasions there is a severe time-lag until receipt. There will once again be a distribution of this time-lag (called lead time) and we can plot this also as shown in Fig. 10.

These are the two basic statistical distributions with which we have to deal in an inventory problem. We shall have to ask the important question about the structure of the costs themselves. How are they related?

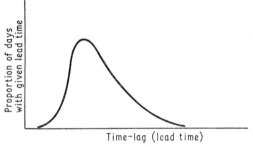

Fig. 10. Statistical distribution of the lead time to meet an order

In the example under discussion we have two categories of cost which are related to the total activity of the inventory system, for, when we look at an inventory situation, we shall find there are certain costs which are associated with the fact that we are *holding* items in stock and there are other costs which are related to the fact that we are *ordering* replacements.

Given the amount of items in stock on any one day we can determine what is the cost of the capital they represent. By this we mean that we take the value of these items and, from the interest rate at which the company values capital, we determine the capital cost per day of holding a given number. Equally a given number of items in stock will provide an estimate of the time period over which they are likely to be held by means of the average daily demand. The average life of items in stock will give an estimate of their obsolescence. If items in store deteriorate according to time we have another type of cost which is associated with the total held. According to the number in store there will, therefore, be a daily cost to be charged which is linearly related to the total number of items held.

On the other hand there are the costs associated with re-

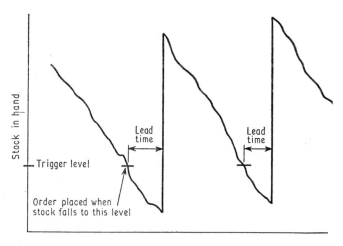

Fig. 11. The variation of inventory with time

ordering items. Every time we transmit an order to the suppliers a clerical cost is incurred. Every time batches of items are received there is a handling cost in transferring them to store, and a billing cost associated with payment. These costs will be related not to the total number of items held in stock but to the total number of times we make an order for replenishment. Hence, we have in the inventory situation one group of costs which increase in proportion to stock held while there is another group which is related to reordering.

Let us consider, then, a typical inventory situation. We shall suppose that we watch the level of stocks held and when it falls to a certain trigger point we shall reorder. After the order is placed there is a lead time until the replacements arrive when the stock held leaps up by the amount that has been received. We have a typical picture of the stocks held in Fig. 11.

We can see that the mechanism of the inventory system depends on two factors only. The first is the level of the trigger point, namely how low we should allow stock to fall before reordering. This will be related to the lead time and the average daily demand. The product of the average lead time and average daily demand will be the average consumption of items during the period we are waiting for an order to be supplied. If there is going to be a charge to us from running out of stock then we must set this reorder point at an appropriately high level. This trigger point therefore is set arbitrarily according to probability statistics and the assessment of the cost of running out of stock and is independent of the other costs. It is a crucial point in the inventory argument, but lies outside the scope of this present discussion. But what of the other variable, which is the reorder quantity? This is certainly at our disposal as a controllable factor and it is something which we can select so as to operate the total scheme to maximum cost efficiency.

Let us now look again at the structure. Over a long period of time, if our reorder quantity is Q and the average daily demand is d, then the time interval between successive reorders will be $\dfrac{Q}{d}$. If the cost of making an order and of all the ancillary work associated with receiving the goods is c, then every $\dfrac{Q}{d}$ days we are going to be subjected to a cost c.

Hence over a period of N days the total number of orders made will be Nd, and the total cost of making orders incurred over the period N days will be $N \times \dfrac{d}{Q} \times c$.

But what of the cost of the stocks held? Over this period of time the average stock held will be $T - dL + \dfrac{Q}{2}$, where T is the trigger point and L is the average lead time. Hence $T - dL$ is the average of the stock on hand when the order is received. If the value of the interest rate gives us a conversion factor K, for the cost of stock in hand, then if we reorder in amounts of Q each time, the total cost of the system over the period of N days will be

Holding cost + Reordering cost

$$= N \times \frac{d}{Q} \times c + N \times \left(T - dL + \frac{Q}{2}\right)K$$

The only controllable factor in this equation is Q. By elementary calculus we can differentiate this cost equation with respect to Q; since Q is the decision variable under study, we obtain

$$0 = -N \times \frac{d}{Q^2} \times c + N \times \frac{K}{2}$$

i.e. $Q^2 = 2\dfrac{d.c}{K}$

$$Q = \sqrt{\left(2\frac{d.c}{K}\right)}$$

Hence the reorder quantity which minimizes the total cost is given by this square root formula.

From this we can see that, deducing the structure of the situation by asking what is going on, we can construct a model which links together the costs we have studied. The important thing about this equation is that we do not have to run the stock control point under different conditions and deduce the costs in each. What we do is to inquire the basic costs, to build up a structure of cause and effect, and to deduce the best solution.

When we study the model more closely we see that it is composed of two basic costs, one of which is represented by the equation

$$\text{Holding cost} = N\left(T - dL + \frac{Q}{2}\right)K$$

which increases as Q increases, while the other is represented by

$$\text{Order cost} = \frac{Ndc}{Q}$$

which decreases as Q increases. The total cost in the model is the sum of these two and the structural relationship of these three costs, namely the two components and their sum, is shown in Fig. 12.

We notice something else about the equation of the model above. We see that on the left-hand side is the objective which we are seeking to optimize, in this case it is the total cost of the system. On the right-hand side are linked together a number of variables and only one of these is controllable by the manager. This is the reorder quantity. There are, however, a number of uncontrollable features present, such as the lead time of the supplier, the interest rate and the average demand, all of which lie beyond the manager's direct control. This is a special case of the general form of the model in O.R. which is an equation of the following type

$$E = f(x_1, x_2, \ldots x_n, y_1, y_2, \ldots y_m)$$

In this equation there are a number of variables, x, which are those which lie within the control of the manager. There are also the variables y which are beyond his control. These are natural variables such as the state of the economy as a whole, actions of competitors, acts of God, or acts of the Board of Directors of one's own company (which often appear equally as acts of God). The variables x and y are linked together by the functional relationship, f. This functional relationship is deduced from our understanding of what

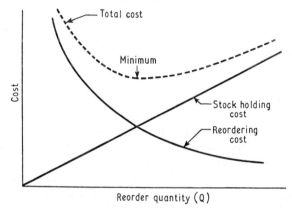

Fig. 12. The make-up of total costs in an inventory situation

is going on in the real-life situation. A simple example of this is the inventory problem which has just been described. Finally the functional relationship is considered against an objective which is the function on the left-hand side of the general model equation.[1] The task of the operational research worker is to forecast the general trend of the variables y, which are the state-of-nature variables, and from an analysis

[1] Strictly speaking this is an objective function, rather than a model. For the time being they can be treated synonymously, but their relationship will be discussed in Chapter XI.

of the functional relationship of these uncontrollables with the controllables x, deduce how the particular set of controllable variables x should be selected to optimize the attainment of the objective on the left-hand side. All this is quite wonderful and ideal in theory. In practice certain snags arise and these we shall deal with in the next chapter.

As can well be imagined problems of the inventory type will arise in very many different kinds of situation and in many different kinds of industry. We are therefore seeing the emergence of the idea that in considering decision-making problems we must distinguish between the form and the content. By the content we mean the general context within which the situation arises and by the form we mean the particular structure of cause and effect which is operating. Inventory problems deal with cause and effect structures which are the linking of a supply and a demand. In general, when inventory problems arise, they are clearly defined and obvious. Hence problems of this form, even though they arise in a variety of contents, are well structured and can be classified fairly rapidly.

On the other hand it is possible for problems of similar form to arise in contents which are sufficiently different to disguise their similarity. Some examples of this will be given in the next chapter but in order to round off this particular chapter on the methodology of model building, we now give three situations all of which have a content which tends to disguise the form and to mask the essential similarities of the equivalence of the three forms.

Consider first of all a convoy of army lorries which is travelling along a road with the objective of moving at a constant speed and with a constant distance between successive vehicles. The first vehicle in the stream may well proceed at this constant speed but we will find that any slight variation in its speed will cause a change in the distance of the second lorry behind it. Any change in the speed of the second lorry will also be translated into a change in the distance between the first two lorries. The result of these two effects is that the variation in speed of the second lorry which is caused, first of all by the natural variation in the speed of the driver and secondly by his attempts to correct the distance he is behind the first vehicle, will be greater than the variability in the speed of the first lorry which consists solely of the natural variability in the driver's speed. Similarly the variability in the speed of the third vehicle will itself be greater than that of the second vehicle because this is compounded of the variability of the third driver's speed together with the variability in speed caused by his compensating for distance. This traverses the length of the convoy, until we get to the last vehicle in the convoy which may well on occasion, if the convoy is long enough, be in the state where it is either racing at 50 m.p.h. in order to catch up the vehicle in front, or is stationary. Anyone who has driven in a convoy of vehicles in traffic is aware of this situation.

The second manifestation of problems of the same structure as this arises in inventory problems themselves.

Consider a chain of units which are both consumers and suppliers where the unit at any level consumes product from the level below and supplies it to the level above as shown in Fig. 13.

The ultimate consumers at the bottom of the pyramid, who are meeting a general steady market demand, will find, as does the first lorry in the convoy, that slight variations in its steady scheme of ordering are translated up the pyramid so that at the last and highest level there is an endemic situation of famine or surplus. The reason for this is the same as in the lorry convoy situation, namely the difficulty of forecasting future demand when there is variability present and the mistake of assuming that at any time the future demand is

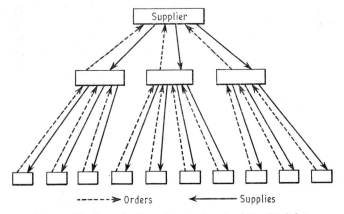

Fig. 13. *The flow of orders and goods through a hierarchical chain*

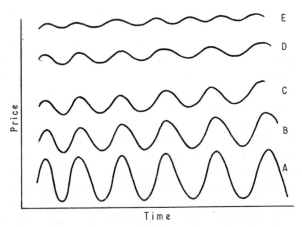

Fig. 14. *Price of product against time, where product flows from A to B to C to D to E the ultimate consumer*

going to be the same as the present. It is this that accounts for the sudden accelerations and decelerations in the lorry convoy, and for the sudden variations in the supply and demand situation down the pyramid for the chain of manufacturers.

The final example of this similar structure stems immediately from the chain of inventory problem. We shall find, for example in many industries, situations which reflect this variation in demand. Let the successive stages in manufacture starting with the raw material and finishing with the consumer market be A, B, C, D and E. If we take the prices at which products are available at these different levels of the industry we will find that whereas the prices for finished goods are fairly steady, being set by the general demand of the public, as we go backwards along the manufacturing chain there is a greater and greater variability until at the raw material end, there is the greatest variability of all. This can be seen in Fig. 14.

The reason for this is the same as in the previous two examples. Hence we see that in three rather different situations we have a decision-making problem which has the same form and, because of this, is manifest in the same symptoms at different levels of the particular situation involved. Clearly control mechanisms have to be designed in the face of structure. This, alas, is rarely done. A full discussion of this will be found in a fascinating book by Beer.[1]

Having seen, then, something of the way in which decision-making models can be constructed, we proceed in the next chapter to study in more detail the way in which we formulate problems and the way in which the form in which problems arise can be classified in certain main structures.

[1] BEER, S., *Decision and Control* (Wiley, 1966).

III

FORMULATION OF PROBLEMS

LET us consider in broad outline the structure of a decision. The first element is a statement of the alternative courses of action from which a choice will be made. The second element is the statement of the consequences of each of these choices. Finally, the third element in the pattern is a statement of the objectives involved. Hence we have these three stages in a decision—choice, consequence, objective.

At first sight this is strange. We are taught by all the good management textbooks that in analysing the consequences of decisions, the first question to ask is: what are the objectives? In his experience, however, the author has found that in an organization one rarely finds the managing director (or the Minister of the Crown), at the foot of the main staircase, standing, like Moses at the foot of Mount Sinai, with tablets of stone on which are engraved the objectives of the organization. It is a curious fact that organizations are largely conducted without a conscious explicit statement of what they are trying to do. Consequently in studying the nature of decision making we firmly place the statement of the objectives as the third member in the trinity. We shall now take these three parts of a decision-making problem in turn and try to see what are the features amongst them which can cause difficulty to the decision maker.

The reason for the existence of O.R. is that in decision making, difficulty arises for the decision maker when either the range of choice is overwhelming, or the consequences of a particular decision are obscure or, finally, there is a lack of knowledge about the objectives, or, more likely, there are many objectives and they cannot be stated on a common scale of values.

There are certain problems in which the range of choice is large. These may be problems in which the consequences of any particular choice are well understood but the arithmetical labour of sorting through the whole range of these is so great that we cannot hope to do so and hence derive an optimum.

Let us take a very simple example of this type. We have a transport fleet which carries goods from two factories to two warehouses. We call these two factories A and B and the warehouses X and Y. We know the cost of shipping one ton of product from each of the factories to each of the warehouses and we know how much is going to be produced at each of the factories each day. How much is needed at each warehouse so as to minimize the total transport cost? We can look at the problem in tabular form.

Cost per Unit Shipped

		To		
		X	Y	
From	A	(5)	(6)	8 Total shipped from A
	B	(3)	(7)	4 Total shipped from B
Total Demand		6	6	Grand Total 12

Note: Costs are always in parentheses.

When we look at this problem we see that there is only one variable available to us. For if the amount which goes from factory A to warehouse X is x, then the amount which goes from factory A to warehouse Y must be $8-x$, the amount which goes from factory B to warehouse X must be $6-x$ and the amount which goes from factory B to warehouse Y will be $x-2$.

D

Hence our problem is to find the amount x which minimizes the total cost of the system and the total cost of the system will therefore be $5x+6(8-x)+3(6-x)+7(x-2)$ which simplifies to $3 . x + 52$. We see that no matter what we do, the cost cannot be less than 52, and as x increases, so does the cost, one unit increase of x increasing the cost by 3.

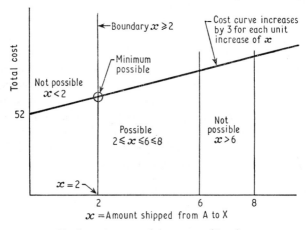

Fig. 15. Total cost in terms of the amount shipped on one route (factory A to warehouse X)

This cost will be a minimum when x is 0. But x cannot be 0 for then the amount which goes from factory B to warehouse Y, which is $x-2$, will be negative, and this is impossible. The traffic which goes along this route, from A to X, shows us that x must be at least 2, in order for there to be a meaningful amount (i.e. an amount at least 0), going from B to Y. Hence we have to minimize the above expression, $3x+52$, with the condition that x is greater than or equal to 2. Also, for similar reasons, x must be less than or equal to 6 and also less than or equal to 8. As the cost increases with x, we must find the smallest allowable value of x. Clearly the condition which satisfies this is $x = 2$, and hence the minimum cost solution is shown in the following table, and the total cost will be $(2 \times 5) + (6 \times 6) + (4 \times 3) + (0 \times 7) = 58$.

	X	Y
A	2(5)	6(6)
B	4(3)	0(7)

This was a straightforward example, because although there is a range of values of x which can be shipped from A to X and hence determine the whole of the transport solution, these values of x must be between 2 and 6. We find that it is possible mathematically to state the whole problem and the total cost is as shown in Fig. 15.

If however we take an example as small as a 3×3 problem, something surprising can happen. Suppose we have three factories, A, B and C and three warehouses, X, Y and Z and the transport costs are given in terms of pounds per ton shipped as in the following table—

		To			
		X	Y	Z	Total Supply
	A	(3)	(7)	(4)	3
From	B	(4)	(9)	(6)	6
	C	(6)	(10)	(9)	5
Total Demand		6	3	5	Total 14

If by the appropriate mathematics we derive the minimum cost for this transportation problem we will find that the methods of common sense are rejected. For common sense would tell us to use as fully as possible the cheapest route, that is to ship all the product from A to X and to avoid the most expensive route which is the route from C to Y. A solution could be built up as shown on page 38.

	X	Y	Z	
A	3(3)	0(7)	0(4)	3
B	3(4)	3(9)	0(6)	6
C	0(6)	0(10)	5(9)	5
	6	3	5	

The cost of this will be

$$(3 \times 3) + (0 \times 7) + (0 \times 4) + (3 \times 4) + (3 \times 9) + (0 \times 6) + (0 \times 6) +$$
$$+ (0 \times 10) + (5 \times 9) = 93.$$

However the minimum cost solution is that shown in the following table, from which it will be seen that the total cost now is 82 units, that is a reduction of about twelve per cent from the common-sense solution.

	X	Y	Z	
A	0(3)	0(7)	3(4)	3
B	4(4)	0(9)	2(6)	6
C	2(6)	3(10)	0(9)	5
	6	3	5	

The curious thing about the minimum cost solution is that it ignores completely the cheapest route and uses quite extensively the most expensive route. For example, we notice that more of the product coming out from factory C goes to the most expensive destination B, than goes to the cheapest destination, which is X for this particular factory. The solution to this problem is calculated by mathematical methods.[1] It can be realized that as these problems increase in size, with more points of production and more destinations, simple graphical methods will break down. We cannot then hope to

[1] SASIENI, M. W., YASPAN, A. and FRIEDMAN, L., *Operations Research* (Wiley).

solve the problem by trial and error or by working through the alternatives for there are too many for us to be able to work through them all, even though the consequence of taking any one of them is exactly known.

A great deal of model building of this type has gone on in many industries which are able to operate in deterministic ways. In the oil industry, for example, the problem of operating a refinery so that the by-products of the crude oil are sold so as to maximize the total profitability of the refinery is one which is fiendishly lengthy to solve by processes of elementary arithmetic. Life is not long enough to sit down and work out all the alternative solutions, even though the consequences of setting a refinery to produce a given range of product in given quantities is completely determined. The British Petroleum Company have derived a series of mathematical models of different aspects of the operation of their whole business incorporating the shipping of oil in tankers from the oil fields to British ports, the decision of how much and what type of crude oil should go through to which refinery, and the market demand for the oil which is processed. When stated explicitly, this problem can involve 1,200 variables linked together by 800 equations and inequalities. Complex as this is, it is possible to take this range of choices and to work through them all by mathematical methods (with extensive help from a computer) and derive a solution which gives a minimum cost or maximum profit. These methods are extremely powerful in a very narrow range of problems. They will tell us with great certainty which course of action must be taken to minimize (or even to maximize) costs. They will tell us what to do in order to minimize or to maximize profits. They will tell us what extra profit we can make if some of the restraints imposed can be related (*see* Chapter V), but they will tell us nothing else. They will not, for example, tell us the second best or the next worst thing to do. In the range of problems of the type in which we are overwhelmed by choice, provided certain mathematical conditions about the relationships of the unknowns are satisfied, methods can be derived for dealing with these aspects. These will also be outlined in Chapter V.

We now consider the second cause of difficulty in decision making, namely that the consequences of a decision are not well known and that we are dealing with doubt and uncertainty. At first sight it is tempting to assume that the methods of hard science have a far greater applicability to the rigid deterministic problem which has just been outlined rather than to those problems in which we are dealing with probability. However the reverse is often true. It is often possible by an analysis of historical data to derive probability measures in a managerial situation. Some examples of this will be given in the chapters which follow, particularly Chapter VII in an example on bidding. We shall for the present content ourselves with remarking that in horse racing the only way to make money (except by being a bookmaker) is to know the true odds on the horse winning and to compare them with the bookmaker's odds. In the real-life situation, if we can evaluate an estimate of a probability, which has some measure of validity associated with it, and compare this with the real cost/pay-off relationship, we can again achieve an important break-through. The methods of operational research therefore have something of importance to say about this general area of variability and probability and this is obviously an area in which we rely heavily on statistical analyses of data.

Finally, we come to the question of the objectives of organizations. There is an arcadian simplicity in assuming that industrial companies are run solely and exclusively to maximize profit or to maximize return on investment (whatever that may mean!). Nothing would be further from the truth. Even the Institute of Directors, that Temple of profit maximization, offers advice to companies on how to spend money on supporting modern artists.

Let us first reflect on the nature of an industrial company. Companies, like all other organizations, are composed of individuals. No individual, unless he is a pretty miserable specimen, goes through life so as to maximize his personal profit and there certainly does not seem to be any rationale in going through life solely to maximize the amount of money we leave to our next of kin. We are all, in our careers, devoted to income but in the sense of an income that will give us a minimum standard of living below which we do not wish to fall. But most individuals can think of firms for which they would not work no matter how much they were paid, simply because these companies or organizations are not the sort with which they would personally want to be associated. The individual therefore is concerned for *status*. In his concern for a minimum salary below which he does not want to fall he is concerned for *survival*. Most individuals could earn more money by changing their job. They do not do so because they are concerned, not only with income, but also with a pattern of relationships within which they are happy to work and which they do not want to take the risk of changing. And so we get the feel of the individual as someone who goes through life trying to maximize his well being, measured in the broadest sense, rather than his *income*. One observes that companies will act as a grand total of the individuals they comprise. Industrial companies are concerned with survival. The answer, for example, to the question of which of the following two equal investments an organization would be willing to undertake, is instructive in this regard.

Investment A is such that we have one chance in two of making £10 million profit and one chance in two of making

£4 million loss. Measured in statistical expectation terms, the expected gain of taking this decision is £3 million profit, that is fifty per cent of £10,000,000 less fifty per cent of £4,000,000.

Investment B is such that there is an absolute certainty of making £1 million profit. Which decision do we take? In most companies one would take decision B, although statistically its expected value is less than decision A. Even if the certain return on decision B declined to half a million, or quarter of a million, or even £100,000, it might well be taken in preference to decision A. For decision A has associated with it a fifty per cent chance of bankruptcy. As survival is the first criterion, this decision will be rejected. But the level at which we take investment A depends on our size, and hence on the utility to us of the sums involved.[1]

An organization is also concerned with its status. This is why companies give money to charity, why they support all sorts of welfare schemes and why they will give money to support universities (for which we are profoundly thankful). Companies also, like an individual, have certain things which they would not dream of doing because they do not act that way. For example, there is a very large American brewing company which manufactures a series of high quality beers. All of these beers are produced, not only because of their contribution to profits, but also because they have been selected by professional brewers as products in which they have pride. A series of studies for this company has shown that substantial further profits could be made if the company would manufacture beers of cheaper price and lower quality. These studies have taken account of the possible loss of image of the company in being associated with a lower grade product, but even so the profit gains would be substantial.

[1] For a discussion of the O.R. approach to investment *see* ADELSON, R. L., Criteria for Capital Investment, *Op. Res. Q.*, March 1965.

Notwithstanding this the company has resolutely refused to countenance any move into the cheaper and lower quality market since they say that as professional brewers they do not want to be associated with poor quality products.

This company is by no means an exception. All organizations, like individuals, have certain things which they do not feel it is their task in life to do and they will not do them even though the individual denies himself extra income, or the company forgoes extra profit. To state the objectives of an organization, therefore, is difficult enough even when we are dealing with one sole unit such as profit, because of the difficulty of determining what is meant by cost, revenue or the time period over which the estimated maximization of profit will take place. The position becomes much more complex when we are dealing with a number of different objectives. The roads programme of this country is bedevilled by the fact that there has been no explicit statement from any government of what it is worth spending to save a life on the roads (although ministries seem to require a minimum number of deaths before they will authorize a zebra crossing). If the amount to be spent could be stated in explicit terms (and what a political argument it would cause) then the derivation of a road safety programme would be much more straightforward.

All companies live with an accident rate which they tolerate. Most organizations are bedevilled by being unsure of the conflict between the profitability they are seeking and the share of market they want to obtain from their sales. Most organizations are unsure of the extent to which they should indulge in welfare schemes for their employees. Most companies will refuse a hire-and-fire policy for labour even though such a policy would give long-term cost savings. The author remembers carrying out a study many years ago in the highly competitive American textile industry where it was explicitly stated by the owner of a group of textile mills that as his mills were the sole source of employment in the communities in which they were located, he was not interested in any solution for raising his profits which would involve him in hiring and firing labour in a cavalier fashion. It is highly fortunate for us all that industry takes this very broad statement of its objectives, for we have eventually to ask the question of what we are here on earth to do.

This was brought home forcibly to the author some time ago when talking to some Lancashire mill owners. He gave them an account of the way in which operational research methods can sometimes lead to increase in profit, and reduction in cost, and at the end of the lecture he was asked a very simple question by a member of the audience. As this man put it, he was the sole owner of the family business. This business was his to run as he liked and he was getting a very nice return out of it, not excessive, but adequate. Why should he bother to do all these other things? He was quite happy as he was and was quite happy to continue the present return on his company's investment. The obvious answer (which did not spring to mind at the time) was that no organization can live in a *status quo*. We have to think in expansive terms, we have to think of dynamic change, of improvements, as otherwise we shall lose staff. Good managers are not interested in staying in an organization which is static, and once good management is lost it is impossible to retain the *status quo*, and the organization will decline. Consequently a company, apart from the moral questions of responsibility to the nation as a whole for the assets entrusted to and administered by it, will find it impossible to do other than seek to maximize its efficiency within the limits of the broad philosophical criteria which it accepts.

We have therefore these three fundamentals of decision making—choice, consequence and objective, and these three are, as can be seen from the previous chapter, linked together by the structural statement of the model.

As has been said the model is a quantified structure within which, by number terms, we link together the pattern of cause and effect relationship obtaining in a decision-making situation. If operational research as a science is to have any cohesive unity these structural relationships must have patterns which operate above and between individual companies. There must be something common in confectionery and in coal mining, in steel making and in soap manufacture, in ship building and in supermarkets which means that the scientific study of the consequences of decisions is something which can be valid away from the particular type of industrial or government setting. Of course, all problems are different, but in order to see the way in which they are different, we have, as stated in Chapter II, to distinguish between the form and the content. By the content of a problem we mean the surface flesh of complexity which is adduced from the surroundings of the particular kind of industry. Hence we will have steel-making problems, coal-mining problems, confectionery problems and so on. But once we get below this surface flesh of complexity, we will find that there is a structure of cause and of probable effect lying behind the particular content within which the form finds itself. All of us, in our own professions, have facets of our job which somehow bring together in one statement, or in one reflection, the whole of our enjoyment. It is often difficult to explain to the outsider why one thing or another should be so enjoyable. So far as the author is concerned, the particular feature of his job as an operational research scientist which gives him delight is the following: on starting to study a management situation one is overwhelmed by complexity, either the complexity of the industry, or of the technological factors, or by the whole of the "noise" of the situation. Gradually, however, by probing, by discussion, by gaining understanding of what is going on one sees emerge from out of this surface flesh of complexity, the skeleton of cause and effect. This is the formal structure of the model and this is what gives the author his own delight. The other intriguing point is that a number of types of structure of problem occur very frequently and that seven main structures account for many of the problems with which one is faced in operational research. Some of these structures will be taken in more detail in the chapters which follow but it is worth while at this stage describing them and showing in some formal flow chart manner the basic elements.

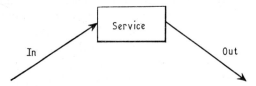

Fig. 16. The structure of a queueing situation

Queueing

The first structure which we take is that which is classified under the heading of queueing problems. The basic structure in queueing is that in which a service is provided to meet a demand. The service facility forms one part of the operation and the other part is provided by the items which are submitted for service.

The structure is shown in Fig. 16.

The task in queueing problems is to provide an optimum balance of service facilities so that the total costs of the operation, namely waiting time in the queue for the items which have come for service and the provision of the service, are minimized. A fuller explanation of queueing problems is given in Chapter IV.

Inventory

The second class of problem, related to queueing, comprises problems with the structure of inventory outlined in the previous chapter. In inventory problems the task is to provide a link in a chain of operations. The link is specifically present to buffer successive stages from variabilities in them. Inventory is a way of relating supply with demand and inventory problems exist when either supply or demand or both are variable. Their basic structure is shown in Fig. 17.

Fig. 17. The structure of an inventory situation

Allocation

The problems which are grouped together under the

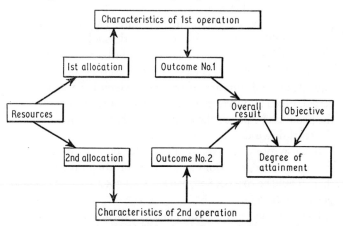

Fig. 18. The structure of an allocation problem

heading of allocation problems are also the subject of Chapter
V. In problems of allocation, we are determining how to
divide limited resources between a number of tasks to which
they can be devoted. The amount of resources devoted to any
given task will yield a pay-off, but in addition there may well
be interactions, so that the total pay-off depends not only on
the separate allocations of resources into the separate tasks
but also on the mixture itself.

The structure of an allocation problem is shown in Fig. 18
(for two tasks only).

Sequencing

Sequencing problems are those in which there is a series of
tasks which have to be carried out and the problem is that of
deciding the order in which these tasks should be performed
so that some factor is either minimized or maximized. The
form of sequencing problem can arise in many separate
contexts and one example of this is now given.

Suppose we have a machine through which different
products can be passed for manufacture. Depending on the
product which has previously gone through the machine
and that which is to follow it, there will be a down time of
the machine which depends on the pairing of products.
Given the total number of products which have to be processed, given also the set of down times, in what order should
the products be passed through the machine so as to minimize
the total down time?

If we wrote down the total number of ways in which as
few as ten products could be scheduled through the machine,
there would be $10 \times 9 \times 8 \times 7 \times 6 \times 5 \times 4 \times 3 \times 2 \times 1 = 3,628,800$
possible schedules.

For each one of these combinations there is a specific total
down time which can be calculated. However we cannot

hope to work through all these in turn and so we derive a mathematical method for solving this particular problem.

This then is one very simple type of sequencing structured problem and is identical with the following: suppose we have a van which has to visit a number of destinations once each; depending on the order of the destinations, there will be a total journey time and the transit time from each of the destinations to each of the others can be tabulated, as the down times were in the example above. The problem here is to work out the sequence of journeys so as to minimize the total journey time and, as can be seen, this is exactly the same structure of problem as the machine sequencing problem, for in this example, journey time corresponds to down time and the origin and the destination of the journey corresponds to the past and future product in the machine.

In recent years, methods have been developed for dealing with sequencing problems which are quite complex. Consider the task of constructing a building. This can be broken down into a number of elementary operations which are such that once an operation is begun, there will be no reason for interrupting it, and so it can be regarded as a unit. For example plastering the inside of a room could be regarded as a unit operation; clearing the ground preparatory to building can be regarded as a unit and so on. If the total task is broken down in this way one can then state logically the dependence of these units on each other in terms of those tasks which have to be completed before others can be begun. A whole building project might then be broken down into perhaps 20,000 different elements and there is a problem involved in deciding the order in which each of these elements should be tackled so that the total task can be performed in minimum time.

Let us look at a small, light-hearted problem which can show the elements of the sequencing method.

Suppose when I get up in the morning I have four basic tasks. One is to shave, the second is to boil water to allow me to shave and also to make the tea, the third is to make toast and the fourth is to cook bacon and eggs and fry bread, which I do by taking the bread and frying it in the fat after I have finished cooking the bacon and eggs. There will be a logic involved in the total series of operations and this logic can be written down in the following flow chart way (times in minutes in parentheses).

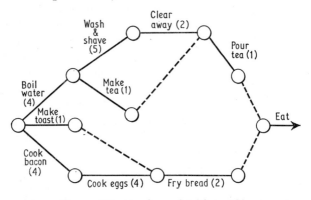

Fig. 19. How to cook your breakfast quickly

Suppose I have to state the particular series of operations which has to be carried out immediately following each other so that the total job is done in minimum time. As can be seen by inspection, the series of operations which are, boil water, shave, clear away shaving kit, pour tea, have a total time associated with them of twelve minutes. This is the longest series from start to finish and hence it is impossible to carry out the whole operation in less than this time. If more than seven minutes are taken from beginning shaving to pouring the tea, this minimum will not be achieved. When the series which is cook bacon, cook eggs, fry and serve cooked food is examined it will be seen that the total time here is ten minutes and this will only take longer if any one of the separate individual units takes longer. In this example, as long as none of the units takes more than one minute longer than is stated, the time to complete the total operation at present will still be twelve minutes. Bread and cooking interact when toast is finished since cooking the fried bread cannot be started until both the bacon and eggs are cooked and the toast is made. The fastest time in which toast can be made is one minute. Hence at the stage at which toast is completed, although it takes one minute, there are seven minutes to spare on these two operations but if more than eight minutes are taken on these two operations the completion of the bacon, eggs and fried bread will inevitably be delayed.

The sequence of operations from boiling water, shaving, clearing away shaving kit and pouring tea is termed critical and the pathway through the simple network which corresponds to that sequence of jobs which have to be performed in immediate succession without interruption in order for the total task to be completed in minimum time is called the critical path. The other operations which are not on the critical path all have slack times associated with them and these slack times give the amount of spare time available within which the operation must be completed in order for the total task to be completed in minimum time.

Simple critical path problems of up to two hundred elements can be solved by inspection or by simple hand methods. When there are more than two hundred elements involved, as very often happens, there are standard computer routines available which will solve these problems, but essentially, as can be seen, the problem here also is one of the sequencing of operations. There are developments of critical path methods which take account of problems in which the time for a task to be completed is not deterministic but is

E

subject to variability. This is an area in which much research has been carried out and some quite impressive improvements in total times for construction work have been achieved by these methods which are becoming standard techniques in the management field.

Search

The problems of search are of a rather different nature. As their name implies, they were originally developed in the

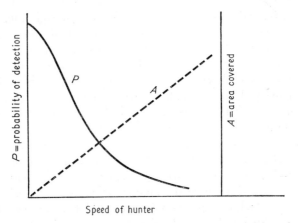

Fig. 20. *The conflict between area covered and probability of detection*

Second World War when one was deploying forces to search for targets, for example the use of aircraft in spotting submarines. One problem which arises here is the relationship between speed of the searcher, area covered, and probability of sighting a target given the speed. Suppose for example the relationship between the probability of a target being observed and the speed of the hunter is as given in Fig. 20.

We can transform this relationship by imposing the increased area covered as a result of the speed being increased and hence as shown in Fig. 21 the optimum speed of the hunter can be derived.

Search problems arise in a number of different guises. The problem of searching for errors in data is one such and this is a typical problem in auditing and accounting generally. In these cases one has to introduce the relationship between the cost of searching for an error and the dividend accruing

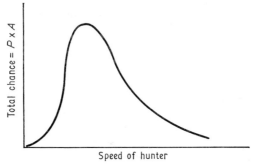

Fig. 21. The chance of detection in terms of the speed of the hunter

from discovering it and so there is a very simple form of cost-benefit relationship to be derived. In supermarkets the opposite problem arises. Here one has the job of so placing goods on the shelves that one will maximize the probability that the shopper will find them. What one is doing here is to manipulate the target so as to maximize its probability of being discovered by the hunter.

Replacement and Maintenance

The problem of replacement and maintenance is concerned with, as the name implies, the relationship between the expenditure on maintaining equipment, compared with its life and, in addition, the problem of replacing equipment in advance of its natural death in order to avoid the costs arising from sudden unexpected breakdown. In these two situations we are concerned basically with statistical questions in which we are using probability to balance between the extremes of two sorts of cost. By their nature most of these problems arise in production processes. They tend to be well structured and have well defined methods available for their solution.

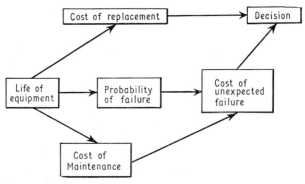

Fig. 22. The structure of a replacement and maintenance problem

Competition

In the area of competition we are extending the nature of the decision-making problem to take account of the existence of opponents as well as nature. We shall be considering problems of competition in rather more detail in Chapter VII. As can be seen in all the problems outlined above, the outcome of a decision is the result of an interaction between the setting of the controllable variables and the occurrence of the uncontrollable variables. We have not introduced the idea of a third set of variables into the model, namely variables under the control of a competitor. In this case the extended form of the model takes the form of

$$E = f(x_1, x_2, \ldots x_n; y_1, y_2, \ldots y_m; z_1, z_2, \ldots z_e)$$

in which the variables grouped under the z notation are those which are at the control of a competitor. We are moreover in the situation in which our objective function and the competitor's objective function are mutually disagreeable, to the extent that the happier we are, the more miserable is our opponent and vice versa. However they are not necessarily equal and opposite. In some competitive marketing situations, for example, the opponents indulge in an escalation of promotional and advertising expense because they have as their main objective the protection of their share of the consumer market, whereas a lower expense all round might lead to higher profits, even at the expense, perhaps, of shedding part of the total market.

These then are the main classes in which the forms of problem arise. As can be seen they are not exhaustive, and it would be possible to fabricate examples which did not fall clearly into any one of these categories. Nevertheless they seem to cover many decision-making problems which arise. The other note of warning, of course, is that it should not be thought that when a problem arises it will be uniquely of one of these structures. The structures themselves overlap and it is a feature of decision-making problems that they break down into a number of sub-problems each of which may be of a different structure. Hence it is not a question, when one is studying these problems of walking round an organization, sniffing the air and saying "Ah, an allocation problem". Life, unfortunately, is not quite as simple as that, as may be seen in some of the chapters which now follow.

IV

QUEUEING PROBLEMS

THE matching of a demand for a service with the provision of the service itself forms the basic structure of the class of problems known as queueing problems. One characteristic of many of these problems is the difficulty of relating together into one statement of an objective the conflicting desires of the server and the served. The following simple example will illustrate this point.

The British operational research worker, R. R. P. Jackson, once had occasion to visit his local doctor daily over a period of some months. He soon discovered that he and the others in the doctor's waiting room were sufferers in more ways than one. It was common to find the waiting room full, and it was common also to have to wait up to two hours in order to see the doctor. He set out to observe what went on and logged the times that different patients took in the doctor's surgery. Some were seen very quickly, they were in and out within a couple of minutes; most took around eight minutes while some took as long as half an hour.

The following example is fabricated, but based on Jackson's study. The general pattern of their consulting times is shown in the table opposite and Fig. 23.

As can be seen from the graph, there is a relatively small chance of either a very short consulting time or a very long consulting time, while there is a gradual build-up from these two extremes to the most popular time of about ten minutes. The doctor in this situation is dealing with an essentially random process. This process is random in two ways: first

Table of One Hundred Observed Consulting Times

Consulting Time (Minutes)	No. of Patients with Observed Consulting Time (Minutes)
4–6	8
6–8	14
8–10	18
10–12	20
12–14	15
14–16	10
16–18	6
18–20	3
20–22	2
22–24	1
24–26	1
26–28	1
28–30	1

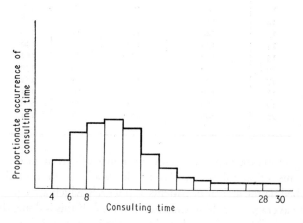

Fig. 23. Statistical distribution of individual patient's consulting time

of all, in that the patients themselves are arriving in his surgery at random intervals of time throughout the consulting period, while it is also random in the sense that the time that the patients take with him varies unpredictably; although, and this must always be remembered, the unpredictability is within an overall pattern.

Patient No.	Patient arrives at (Time From Zero (Mins))	Patient Sees Doctor at	Consulting Time	Patient Leaves Doctor
1	0	0	6	6
2	10	10	14	24
3	20	24	12	36
4	30	36	12	48
5	40	48	8	56
6	50	56	4	60
7	60	60	6	66
8	70	70	8	78
9	80	80	10	90
10	90	90	10	100
11	100	100	8	108
12	110	110	8	118
13	120	120	12	132
14	130	132	8	140
15	140	140	24	164
16	150	164	6	170
17	160	170	14	184
18	170	184	10	194
19	180	194	12	206
20	190	206	8	214

Jackson then considered the possibility of deriving different forms of appointment system. It would seem logical to schedule the arrival of patients at intervals which are equal to the average consulting time (ten minutes). If this is done, then there will be periods when the doctor is unoccupied because he has dealt with his last patient in less than average time and the next patient has not yet arrived. The example (page 58) has been obtained by placing in a box pieces of paper on each of which is a consulting time. All these consulting times when listed would fall into the pattern of the distribution shown in Fig. 23. Taking consulting times at random from the above distribution and, assuming patients arrive exactly on time, it can be seen that there are periods when the doctor has nothing to do. It will also be seen that there are periods when an incoming patient has to wait because the previous patient is taking longer than the average consulting time.

From the small sample of twenty "typical" patients processing through the system in this way (shown in the table on page 58), we can see that the average time a patient has to wait is the average of the separate waiting times, namely—

0, 0, 4, 6, 8, 6, 0, 0, 0, 0, 0, 0, 0, 2, 0, 14, 10, 14, 14, 6

The average wait is 4 minutes.
On the other hand, this low wait is only achieved by the doctor's being idle a total of—

4+4+2+2+2 = 14 minutes.

If two patients, instead of one, were scheduled in at the beginning of the consulting shift, and then one further patient every ten minutes, the same experiment could be carried out. The resulting table is given on page 60.

As can be expected, the average waiting time of a patient has increased while the idle time of the doctor has decreased. The former has moved from 4 to 6·2 minutes, while the latter has moved from 14 to 4 minutes.

With three patients arriving initially and the remainder at 10-minute intervals, a similar experiment on the same data as tabled would give no idle time for the doctor and a patient's average wait of 14 minutes.

Fig. 24 shows clearly the manner in which the interests of

Patient No.	Patient Arrived at	Patient Sees Doctor at	Consulting Time	Patient Leaves Doctor
1	0	0	6	6
2	0	6	14	20
3	10	20	12	32
4	20	32	12	44
5	30	44	8	52
6	40	42	4	56
7	50	56	6	62
8	60	62	8	70
9	70	70	10	80
10	80	80	10	90
11	90	90	8	98
12	100	100	8	108
13	110	110	12	122
14	120	122	8	130
15	130	130	24	154
16	140	154	6	160
17	150	160	14	174
18	160	174	10	184
19	170	184	12	196
20	180	196	8	204

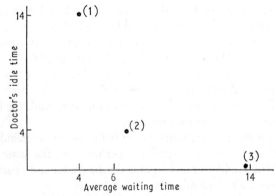

Fig. 24. Idle time of doctor in terms of the initial stock of patients

the patient, who wants a short waiting time, and that of the doctor, who wants full occupancy of his time, will run counter to each other. In many management systems the same problem arises, and in a much more serious way. The problem is that the person who provides the service wants full occupancy of his serving point, in order to get the maximum return on his capital, while the person who is being served does not want to have time wasted in a queue. In the major example which follows in this chapter this point is made quite clearly.

First of all, however, suppose that it is not possible to schedule arrivals, and that the arrival intervals vary. It is tempting to assume that if the average interval between the random arrivals is equal to the average service time of the service operation then the total system will be in balance. This has been one of the great fallacies of production management. Let us take an example of the type which the reader can also fabricate.

Consider a simple situation in which items arrive for service at random intervals of time, the average of the intervals being 50 minutes and the range being from 5 to 90 minutes. Let us take a "typical" example of this with a randomly arranged set of 20 arrival intervals which have the assigned minimum, average, and maximum values (*see* table on page 62). We take also a set of service times of the same nature, that is average 50 and range, 5 to 90. (Perhaps the reader will take it on trust that these are samples taken at random by the author from distributions with these characteristics. This accounts for the slight divergence of the averages of the two sets of twenty numbers neither of which is exactly 50.)

The figure of 93 per cent is a little misleading. The whole of the idle time at the service point occurs in three of the first four arrivals. For all others after the fourth, there is no idle time and the waiting time increases steadily. As can be seen, by the time item 20 arrives, items 18 and 19 are still in the queue. If we carried on the experiment long enough, the queue length would increase indefinitely.

Item No.	Arrival Interval	Arrival Time	Service Time	Time In	Time Out	Waiting Time	Idle time of Server
1	30	30	40	30	70	0	30
2	65	95	50	95	145	0	25
3	50	145	30	145	175	0	0
4	50	195	70	195	265	0	20
5	20	215	35	265	290	50	0
6	60	275	70	295	365	15	0
7	45	320	85	365	450	45	0
8	55	375	40	450	490	75	0
9	55	430	50	490	540	60	0
10	15	445	80	540	620	95	0
11	50	495	50	620	670	125	0
12	85	580	30	670	700	90	0
13	40	620	60	700	760	80	0
14	90	710	40	760	800	50	0
15	45	755	90	800	890	45	0
16	5	760	25	890	915	130	0
17	40	800	75	915	990	115	0
18	60	860	55	990	1,045	130	0
19	50	910	45	1,045	1,090	135	0
20	70	980	10	1,090	1,100	110	0

Average waiting time over first 20 arrivals $= \dfrac{1,350}{20} = 67$

Total idle time of server over first 20 arrivals = 80 minutes,

i.e. occupancy of service point $= \dfrac{1,140 - 80}{1,140} = 93$ per cent

If the situation is now placed more in favour of the arrivals by spreading them out (this is equivalent to reducing the service times) the reader can check the improvement (from the arrival's viewpoint) by adding 5 to each arrival interval in the table on page 62 and recalculating the average waiting time and the total idle time of the server. If he does this also by adding 10, 15 to the arrival intervals he will derive the following results—

Average Service time = 50		
Average Interval Between Arrivals	Average Waiting Time	Percentage Occupancy of Service Point
50	67	93
55	39	91
60	24	86
65	15	79

There are a number of examples of production line facilities which are created to meet an essentially random demand upon them, where the average time needed in the production line to carry out an operation on the incoming units is equal to the random interval of arrival between successive units. When this occurs, management have always been surprised that this system seems to lead to constant overtime and constant expediting of jobs at great cost. Successive production managers have been chided for being unable to meet the arrival pattern when they are provided with systems which are in balance with this pattern. However, such a balancing is not a passport to efficiency but rather to chaos. It is an interesting commentary on mathematical research in this general problem area, that it was only when queueing theory was formally worked out as a subject that it was realized why such a system does lead to chaos. It is possible by means of the mathematical theory of queues to work out the average length of a queue in terms of the average interval between random arrivals and the average service time (the formula which follows assumes certain characteristics of the statistical distribution of the arrival and of the service time, but reference to this fuller treatment is made at the end of the chapter). The average waiting time will be $\dfrac{S^2}{A-S}$, where A is the average interval between arrivals and S is the average time of service. As can be seen from this formula, when the average arrival interval and the average service time are equal, the average length of the queue of items waiting for service is infinite.

The reason for this is not hard to seek and can be seen exposed in the numerical example above.

The fallacy in the argument which assumes that this system will lead to a balance is based on the assumption that what we are doing in relating these averages is to take a very large number of service time intervals and add them up, and see how they match with a very large number of arrival time intervals. Of course, if the averages of the two distributions of service time and of arrival interval are equal, then the sum of a large number of arrival times will equal the sum of a large number of service times. But, we can only carry out a service when there is something in the queue. Consequently we are not matching successive items from two distributions. We can only take something from the service time distribution when there is already something waiting, and so where these two averages are equal we will be building up a situation in which the average queue length will get greater and greater.

One of the classical queueing problems was studied some years ago by Eddison and Owen.[1] Their study was part of an investigation of the total system of importing iron ore from the overseas dockside to the blast furnace bunkers in Britain. The queueing problem which formed part of this study was to discover what should be done to lower the total

[1] Discharging Iron Ore, *Op. Res. Q.* September, 1953.

cost of transporting ore from overseas port to unloading wharf and to balance the savings and losses. This total cost can be divided into two parts—

    1. The shipping cost—this is the cost of the sea journey plus the value of the time spent in the loading port.

    2. The total cost of discharge, which includes the cost of operating the unloading installation plus the value of the time ships spend in the unloading port.

This problem, as tackled by Eddison and Owen, formed an admirable example of the way in which the structure of a decision-making problem is evolved. The first study of the investigation was to list the controllable and the uncontrollable factors and to show in flow chart form, the way in which they affect each other. It is this approach which distinguishes the operational research method from the attempt to resolve problems by a mixture of argument and accountancy. As we have said earlier, the words of the English language cannot deal adequately with this sort of situation and, as can be seen, Fig. 25 presents and discusses the amount of information it contains infinitely more economically and efficiently than would be possible in terms of a straight English language translation.

In Fig. 25 the factors which are in rectangles are those which are controllable, although they cannot all be varied independently of each other in practice. The oval frames are for factors in the unloading ports which vary as a rule of choosing different values of the controllable factors.

The essence of a situation such as this is that it is not possible to experiment in real-life terms. All that is available in real life is a particular set of observations carried out under a particular set of conditions, together with some estimates of costs in other situations. These are the only quantitative data which feed into the analysis and these data, together with the

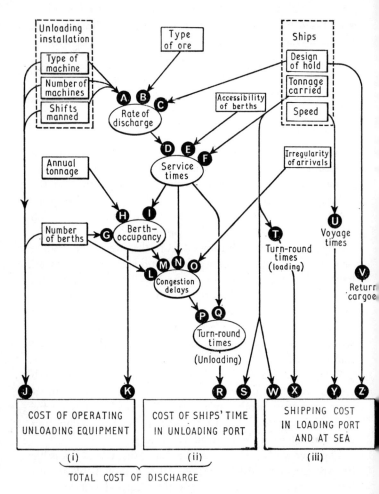

Fig. 25. The flow chart of cause and effect in a ship docking problem
(Reproduced by courtesy of the Editor, *Operational Research Quarterly*)

(i) Cost of Operating Unloading Equipment

Rate of discharge depends on (A) features of the installation,

                      (B) type of ore,

         and (C) design of the ships' holds.

Service times   depend on (D) rate of discharge,

                      (E) accessibility of the berth (i.e., time taken to approach and leave berth),

         and (F) tonnage carried by the ship.

Berth occupancy depends on (G) number of berths at the port,

                      (H) annual tonnage handled,

         and (I) service-time.

The cost of operating the unloading equipment depends on (J) the installation,

         and (K) the use made of it, berth-occupancy.

(ii) Cost of Ships' Time in Unloading Port

Congestion delays depend on (L) number of berths,

                      (M) berth-occupancy,

                      (N) mean service-time,

         and (O) irregularity of ship-arrivals.

Turn Round Times are the sum of (P) delays,

         and (Q) service-times.

The cost of ships' time in the unloading port depends on (R) turn-round-time,

         and (S) size of ship.

(The sum of (i) and (ii) above is the *total cost of discharge*)

(iii) Shipping Cost (in Loading Port and at Sea)

In comparisons of different types of ship on some particular voyage:

Turn round time depends on (T) the tonnage loaded.

Voyage time   depends on (U) speed of ship.

Return cargoes the possibility of using ships for this purpose depends on (V) design of hold.

Shipping cost (loading and at sea) depends on (W) size of ship,

                      (X) turn-round-time (loading),

                      (Y) voyage-time,

         and (Z) whether a return cargo is carried.

logic expressed in the above diagram, are sufficient to solve the problem.

The data which were obtained fell into four groups—

1. The effects of unloading installation, type of ore and ship design on the rates of discharge. These are the factors at the top of Fig. 25.

2. The prediction of congestion delays and turn-round times for various values of service time and berth occupancy.

3. The costing of unloading and ship's time.

4. The determination of shipping cost at sea dependent on the type of ship used.

A fuller description of the way in which these data were obtained is given by Eddison and Owen. The central point was that the arrival of ships at ports can be regarded as random to a large extent. It is therefore possible to use queueing theory to enable the average congestion delay per ship to be predicted for each port, from a knowledge of the number of berths, the service time, and the berth occupancy. This latter statistic is defined as the proportion of time that a berth is actually occupied by a ship being discharged.

There are two ways in which the theory can be used. First it is possible to use theoretical results to check back over the period for which data have been collected to see whether what has been happening confirms the results of the theoretical study. If so, and in fact it was so, one can then use the theory with a certain amount of confidence to predict for the future.

Now queueing theory is a mathematical approach to the problem of estimating the relationship between the amount of time which incoming items will wait in a queue in terms of the arrival time distribution (that is the distribution of the time between successive arrivals in the queue), the pattern of service times and the number of service points. In the present situation the arrival time distribution was effectively random

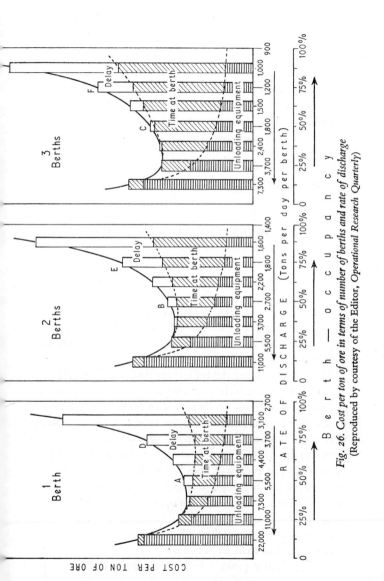

Fig. 26. Cost per ton of ore in terms of number of berths and rate of discharge
(Reproduced by courtesy of the Editor, Operational Research Quarterly)

and hence it could be fed directly into the algebra of queueing theory. The service time distribution was estimated by taking different sorts of unloading equipment, giving known rates of discharge, measured in tons per day per berth. The way in which the cost per ton of ore for a typical port discharging one million tons of ore per year from 8,000-ton tramp vessels would vary was calculated and is shown in Fig. 26.

As can be seen from the one-berth graph, the cost of the unloading equipment increases as the rate of discharge increases, but the time at the berth decreases and so do the delays to ships waiting to enter the port. Hence these graphs then gave for the one-berth, two-berth and three-berth situations, the optimum rate of discharge to be aimed at in order to minimize the total costs of the discharge.

Of course, for different figures of total annual tonnage through the port the optimum number of berths will vary and so will the optimum form of the unloading equipment. Fig. 27 shows the way in which, in terms of a different tonnage through a port, the type of unloading equipment and the number of berths can be selected so as to minimize total cost.

These graphs show the typical conflict which develops in a queueing situation. If the port operator measures his efficiency in terms of the berth occupancy then he will only be highly productive in situations where the total cost of the system is very high. This can be seen in the one-berth, two-berth and three-berth figures (Fig. 27) where a berth occupancy figure of over 90 per cent will coincide with a situation in which the time at berth is high and in which the cost of delays is very high. In fact the berth occupancy figure corresponding with an overall optimization will never be as high as 90 per cent and for modest values of annual tonnage through the port will be less than 50 per cent.

One particular point which stems from this is the peril

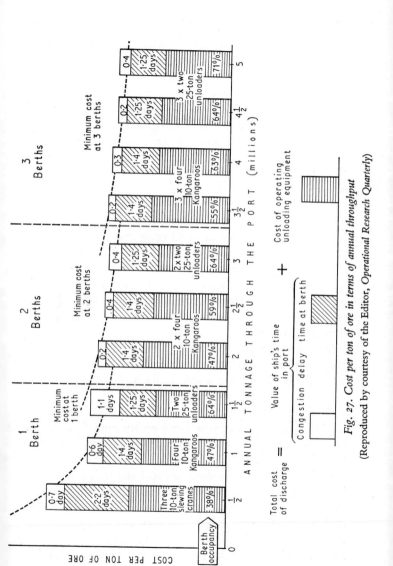

Fig. 27. Cost per ton of ore in terms of annual throughput
(Reproduced by courtesy of the Editor, Operational Research Quarterly)

which lies in trying to use a productivity measure which applies only to a part of a system as a way of judging the efficiency of the whole. In practice, of course, it is difficult to link together the two parts of the shipping operation. Sometimes this can be done by formulating a system of bonus payments which may link together the interests of the port operator and the ship owner. For example, the ship owner may pay a bonus to the port operator in terms of the total turn-round times and this operates in a number of ports.

This particular problem was solved mathematically by queueing theory, an excellent account of which is given by Lee.[1] In more complex cases however the queueing theory approach breaks down and one then has to make an approach through simulation. Simulation will be discussed in Chapter VIII and a simple example of simulation was given at the beginning of this chapter with the doctor's appointments system. However we can see how this can apply to the shipping problem.

Suppose we introduced other variables into the problem. For example, a port may only be accessible during periods when the level of water is sufficiently high for ships to have access to the dock. In this case we have imposed another variable which means that the approach through mathematical queueing theory is considerably complicated. We could then, as in the doctor's waiting room problem, run a hypothetical port by paper and pencil. What one would do would be to take a long sheet of paper and to impose on the horizontal axis a time scale on which would be indicated the periods during which there would be sufficient water to enable a ship to enter or leave the port. One would then take the arrival time distribution and sample from it at random and then impose on the piece of paper at the appropriate time intervals the instants at which a ship has arrived outside the port. The port can then be operated for any number of berths as an experiment. Ships would be fed in, unloaded with the appropriate random sample times from service time distribution and then, when the tide allows, they can leave the berth free for a successor. As can be seen, in these terms it would be possible to experiment with different rates of arrival, different sizes of ship, different rates of discharge (with different costs for the unloading equipment) and in addition, to interlock with these factors the effect on the economics of the overall system of dredging the channel to different depths to give greater access to the port. These methods clearly have great power and were actually used in further investigations following the work on queueing described earlier. They provide a way of avoiding the real-life time and cost associated with actual experiments and are clearly a bridge between the O.R. scientist and the laboratory scientist, who also sets up experiments and gains experience from the experimental method.

A Do It Yourself Queueing Kit

The reader might like to try some queueing experiments for himself. This can be done quite easily by using a pair of dice to generate arrival interval and service times.

Total 2	will occur on average	1 in 36 times				
3	,,	,,	2	,,	,,	,,
4	,,	,,	3	,,	,,	,,
5	,,	,,	4	,,	,,	,,
6	,,	,,	5	,,	,,	,,
7	,,	,,	6	,,	,,	,,
8	,,	,,	5	,,	,,	,,
9	,,	,,	4	,,	,,	,,
10	,,	,,	3	,,	,,	,,
11	,,	,,	2	,,	,,	,,
12	,,	,,	1	,,	,,	,,

If two dice are thrown the frequency with which the possible totals, 2, 3, 4, 5, 6, 7, 8, 9, 10, 11 and 12, will occur are shown in the table on page 73.

The following is an example of how to estimate the service point occupancy, the average queueing time, and the probability of waiting longer than any assigned time, for a given combination of arrival and service time—

Assume arrival interval averages 10, with a range of 6 to 14.

Assume service time averages 8, with a range of 4 to 12.

Then throw pairs of dice to represent in turn the arrival interval and service time and allocate the total as follows—

Dice total	Arrival Interval	Expected Frequency Percentage
2, 3	6	3/36 = 8
4, 5	8	20
6, 7, 8	10	44
9, 10	12	20
11, 12	14	8

and

Dice total	Service Time	Expected Frequency Percentage
2	4	3
3, 4, 5	6	25
6, 7, 8	8	44
9, 10, 11	10	25
12	12	3

The reader can formulate different allocations of dice totals, provided the average service time, or arrival interval expected, is at the average required. The average expected is obtained by adding the products of the interval (or service time) and the frequency with which it is expected to occur. For example, the average arrival interval above will be

$6 \times 0.08 + 8 \times 0.20 + 10 \times 0.44 + 12 \times 0.20 + 14 \times 0.08 =$
$$= 0.48 + 1.6 + 4.4 + 2.4 + 1.12 = 10.0$$

The experiment might begin as follows—

1st arrival time dice throw gives	4+3,	i.e. arrival interval of 10
1st service time ,,	,,	,,	2+2,	i.e. service interval of 6
2nd arrival time ,,	,,	,,	1+2,	i.e. arrival interval of 6
2nd service time ,,	,,	,,	6+5,	i.e. service interval of 10
3rd arrival time ,,	,,	,,	1+1,	i.e. arrival interval of 6
3rd service time ,,	,,	,,	5+4,	i.e. service interval of 10

etc.

and the data sheet would appear as—

Item	Arrives at	Into service at	Out from Service at	Idle time of service Point	Time waiting in Queue
1	10	10	10+ 6 = 16	10	0
2	10+6 = 16	16	16+10 = 26	0	0
3	16+6 = 22	26	26+10 = 36	0	4
etc.	etc.	etc.	etc.	etc.	etc.

A run of about one hundred items will give a good estimate of the percentage occupancy of the service point and the average time waiting in the queue. These experiments can be refined to deal with all the variants of the queueing problem—

Arrival interval

Service time

Number of service channels: how many service points are there?

Queue discipline: do some arrivals automatically go to the head of the queue; do those waiting in the queue get discouraged and leave after a given time, etc?

V

ALLOCATION PROBLEMS

ALLOCATION problems fall into three main categories. We shall discuss first of all the simplest type and then two more complex types which are obtained by removing restrictions which obtain in the simplest case.

The simplest allocation problem is defined by the following conditions—

1. There is a set of jobs to be done.

2. Enough resources are available for doing all of these jobs.

3. At least some of the jobs can be done in different ways and hence by using different amounts and combinations of resources.

4. Some of the ways of doing these jobs are better than others (that is, are less costly or more profitable).

5. There are not enough resources available to do each job in the best way.

The task in the simplest of the allocation problems is to divide resources among jobs in such a way that some objective is achieved at an extreme, that is either cost is minimized or profit maximized. An example of this is a number of jobs, each of which requires one and only one resource. If the number of jobs and the number of resources are equal we can draw up a table to show the way in which we have assigned resources against jobs.

As a simple example, suppose we have four machines to

extract mineral from an ore and the efficiency of extractions are—

Machine A. Efficiency 70 per cent
Machine B. Efficiency 50 per cent
Machine C. Efficiency 50 per cent
Machine D. Efficiency 40 per cent

We also have four amounts of material—

1. 6,000 tons   3. 4,000 tons
2. 5,000 tons   4. 3,000 tons

Which material should be allocated to which machine so as to maximize the total yield?

Machine	Material			
	1	2	3	4
	6,000	5,000	4,000	3,000
A 70%	4,200	3,500	2,800	2,100
B 50%	3,000	2,500	2,000	1,500
C 50%	3,000	2,500	2,000	1,500
D 40%	2,400	2,000	1,600	1,200

The problem is to select four of the sixteen squares, one in each row and one in each column so that the product of row efficiency and column total, given in each square, is maximized. Standard methods are available for this type of problem.

A rather more complex type of problem is that in which each job can be performed by more than one resource and each resource can be deployed on more than one job. A simple example of this is the 3 × 3 transportation problem which was discussed in Chapter III. Referring to the quantities used in that example, mathematically we had to find nine numbers, one corresponding to each of the nine possible

[1] SASIENI, M. W., YASPAN, A. and FRIEDMAN, L., *Operations Research Problems* (Wiley).

routes (three origins to three destinations) so that the transport cost is minimized while at the same time the right amounts are shipped out of each factory and into each warehouse. Let these amounts be as given in the following table—

	X	Y	Z	Total
A	a	b	c	3
B	d	e	f	6
C	g	h	i	5
Total	6	3	5	

The requirements stated in mathematical terms are—

minimize $C = 3a + 7b + 4c + 4d + 9e + 6f + 6g + 10h + 9i$

subject to: (i) $a + b + c = 3$
(ii) $d + e + f = 6$
(iii) $g + h + i = 5$
(iv) $a + d + g = 6$
(v) $b + e + h = 3$
(vi) $c + f + i = 5$

It will be noticed that all the equations are simple in nature. There are no squared terms; that is we do not have anywhere terms such as x^2. There are no square root terms. Every one of the nine quantities which we have to find is related by a number of equations which could be drawn in terms of straight lines. There are standard methods for solving this sort of problem and they form part of the whole network of methods called linear programming. It is not in the nature of this book to indicate the way in which such a solution is worked out, but mathematically it can be determined that the minimum cost solution to the above transportation problem is as given on page 38, Chapter III.

This result corresponded to a total cost of 82 and no matter what route is taken the transportation cannot be achieved at a lower cost than this. It was noticed that the result was quite surprising. Clearly in a situation such as this, it would be wrong to judge either the factory manager by the cost of the shipments made from his factory or to cost the warehouse by the cost of the shipments it receives. The minimization of the whole does not correspond with minimizing the transport cost involved in each of the separate warehouses and factories. This is an important truth which is part of a general statement made from time to time in this book.

In general, transportation problems are rather more complex and the fact that in even a simple example we get a strange answer will alert us to the knowledge that in the more complex cases the solution is even less straight-forward.

The National Coal Board some years ago carried out an investigation in one of its areas of the costs of transporting coal from collieries to washeries to coke ovens. In each of the fifteen collieries concerned there was a total amount of coal which could be produced and this coal was divided among different grades and sizes. At each colliery, there was a limitation on the amount of coal which could be shipped out each day by road and rail. Each washery had a total amount of coal which it could process each day and also had a limitation on the amounts of coal it could receive and that it could ship out each day. Finally each coke oven had certain demands each day for the amounts of coal to be received by grade and by size as well as a restriction on the total it could receive.

Given the transportation costs of coal from each colliery to each washery and from each washery to each coke oven, how much should be shipped each day in order to minimize these transport costs? This problem needs the standard technique of linear programming. The complexity of these problems is such that, in terms of the minimum costs solution, the restrictions are never all operative. Hence, in this case, the solution will be such that at least one of the amounts to be shipped or received will be at the particular capacity restriction involved. In general the solution shows that some restrictions are not restrictions at all, when the optimum solution is found while others are operative and will be costing money. This point is made in the following example from the textile industry.

We shall now consider problems of production which have the same basic structure as the allocation problems which we are discussing. Once again let us start with a simple problem. We have two products A and B which in order to be manufactured have to pass successively through two machines 1 and 2. The amount of time that one unit of product takes in passing through each of the two machines differs. The number of hours that one unit of products A and B respectively take on machine 1 are 8 and 3 hours. The number of hours that one unit of products A and B takes on machine 2 are respectively 4 and 6 hours. We are also told that there are 24 hours available each day on each of the two machines, while the contribution to profit of selling one unit of product A is £5 and one unit of product B is £3. The question to answer is: how much of each product should be made in order to maximize the total contribution to profit? (In this simple example we are of course ignoring overheads, labour, depreciation, rent and so on, all of which we shall regard as constant irrespective of the balance of product made. This is not an unreasonable assumption.)

It is possible to solve this sort of problem in graphical form. For example, if we take a sheet and rule it out as shown opposite, we shall take the horizontal axis as the number of units of product A we are going to make and we shall take the vertical axis as the number of units of product B. We can now draw on the graph two lines which represent restrictions made on us by machine capacity. If we produce x of product A and y of product B, the total amount of time which is spent on machine 1 in doing so will be 8 hours for every one of the x units, and 3 hours for every one of the y units. The total time will be $8x + 3y$, and we are told that this must not exceed 24. Hence if we draw a line joining a point 3 units along the machine A axis to the point 8 units up the machine B axis, all possible combinations of amounts to be produced are represented by points on this graph lying below and to the left of this line.

Similarly for machine 2. This also has 24 hours of capacity available and all possible combinations of product A and B which can be made are represented on the graph by points lying below and to the left of the line joining a point 6 units

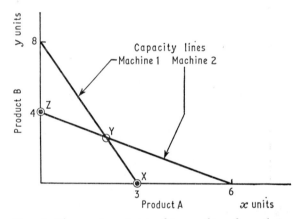

Fig. 28. The capacity restraints of two machines for producing different combinations of the two products

along the machine A axis to a point 4 units vertically up the product B axis. (The reader can check for himself that any point lying below and to the left of the line representing the capacity of machine 1 will correspond to a total time demand on machine 1 of less than 24.)

In order to satisfy the capacity restraint of 24 hours' time available on both machine 1 and machine 2, the combinations of amounts of products A and B which can be made lie within the four-sided figure bounded by the axes and *XY,YZ*.

We now have to find the particular combination of amounts of product to be made which maximizes profit, that is the particular point within this four-sided figure which corresponds to maximum profit.

Look at the profit statement. The contribution to profit from 1 unit of product A is £5 and from 1 unit of product B is £3. Consequently if we make x units of product A and y units of product B our total profit will be

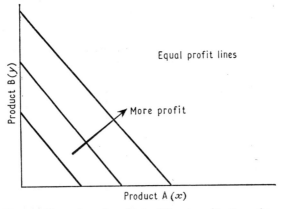

Fig. 29. *Lines of equal profit for different combinations of two products*

$5x + 3y$. All combinations of amounts of A and B which can be made, for which their total profit is the same, are represented by points on parallel straight lines. For example, if we make £10 profit then the amount of A we make and the amount of B can either be 2 and 0 respectively, 0, and $3\frac{1}{3}$ respectively, or 1 and $1\frac{2}{3}$ respectively and so on. In these three examples, the profit will always be £10. These three points lie on the straight line which joins a point lying 3 units along the A axis to a point lying 5 units up the B axis (Fig. 29). All combinations of product to be made which make a profit of £10 are represented by points lying on this straight line. On the other hand if we want to make a profit of £20, this can be achieved by making 4 units of product A and 0 of B, or 0 of A and 6⅔ of B, or alternatively any other combination which lies on the line joining a point 4 units along the A axis to a point 6⅔ units up the B axis. These two lines, that is the £10 profit line and the £20 profit line, are parallel and, in fact, all lines of equal profit will be parallel.

We have to find a point lying within the four-sided figure of Fig. 28 which lies as far as possible upwards and to the right on one of the equal profit lines, for as we move up and to the right we find ourselves on lines which represent more and more profit. What we do is place Fig. 29 on top of Fig. 28 and look for the point where profit is greatest. This corresponds to the point Y. At this point the amounts of A and B we make are 2 and ⅔ respectively. This corresponds to a profit of £18. This is the most profit we can make.

Once again we notice, in this situation, all the lines we have drawn to represent the things that we can do are straight lines. The straight lines represented the capacities of machines 1 and 2 and translated these capacities into comparable amounts of products A and B that it was feasible for us to make. A straight line represented points of equal profitability. Hence to maximize profitability we are again in a situation where we can use linear programming methods. In this particular example we did not need to go to any advanced algebra because the problem could be solved graphically.

We can also deduce other things about this particular problem, by studying these graphs carefully. If the profitability of A is more than ⅔ times as great as B, the parallel straight lines will be such that the point representing maximum profitability will be the point X. This means that once A becomes more than ⅔ times more profitable than B we would make only X. In this situation, machine 1 will be working to capacity and machine 2 will only be working at fifty per cent of capacity. On the other hand if B is more than two-thirds as profitable as A, the best point from this set of parallel straight lines will be Z. In this situation, we will make only B and we will make 4 units of it. This will correspond to twenty-four hours a day usage on machine 2 but only twelve hours a day usage on machine 1, and so there will be only fifty per cent capacity used on the second machine. We can, therefore, in terms of the relative profitability of the two products show what we should make as in the following table.

Profitability of A compared with B	Optimum amount of		Capacity Used in Machine (per cent)	
	A	B	1	2
More than $\frac{8}{3}$ times	3	0	100	50
Between $\frac{8}{3}$ and $\frac{2}{3}$ times	2	$\frac{8}{3}$	100	100
Less than $\frac{2}{3}$ times	0	4	50	100

Further study of the graph will show even more. Let us take the situation as outlined in the table above. We ask what extra profit we could make if we were able to produce more capacity on machine 1 or machine 2. We can generalize this question to ask whether, if the costs of obtaining slightly more capacity on machine 1 are different from those of getting slightly more capacity on machine 2, in which of these machines would it be more profitable to invest? This answer we also work out in graphical form. We take the restraint represented by machine 1, move it slightly upwards and to the right and find out what would be the extra profit made if we had, say, 1 hour more capacity on this machine. In this case we would have the two lines as shown in Fig. 30 and it can be seen that the extra profit corresponding to this change in capacity would be £0·5. On the other hand, if we kept machine 1 capacity at 24 hours and increased machine 2 by

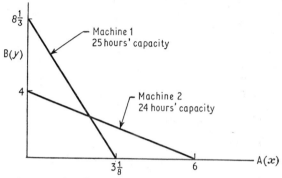

Fig. 30. *The effect of creating extra capacity on machine 1*

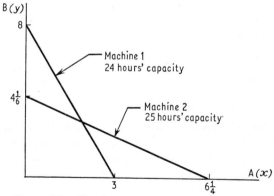

Fig. 31. *The effect of creating extra capacity on machine 2*

another hour, that is to 25 hours, then we would have an extra profit of £0·25. From this it is seen that it is better, in this circumstance, to invest the extra money on machine 1 rather than machine 2.

We can introduce further restraints. It may be that there are restrictions applied in the market to the amounts of products A and B that we can sell. Suppose that in the table on page 84 we had the additional restraint that the total amount of product A which we could possibly sell any day was $2\frac{1}{2}$ units and the total amount of product B which we could sell any day was 2 units. This would correspond to the two extra lines, one vertical and one horizontal shown in Fig. 32.

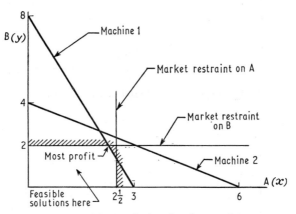

Fig. 32. The introduction of market restraints

In these circumstances it can be seen that the maximum profit solution of £$17\frac{1}{4}$ corresponds to making $2\frac{1}{4}$ units of A and 2 units of B, and so the introduction of this market restraint has reduced the previous maximum profit by 15s.

The Three Machine Case

By a similar method we can treat any number of machines as long as the total number of products remains at 2. For each machine which we consider we shall introduce another straight line of the form of the restraints for machines 1 and 2 in Fig. 28. When we do this we shall generally find that the optimum profit solution does not correspond with all three machines working to capacity. To illustrate this, suppose the demands made by products A and B on machines 1 and 2 are as given above, but the demands on machine 3 are 6 hours of machine time for each unit of product A and $\frac{24}{5}$ hours of machine time for each unit of product B. This introduces a third line on the graph of machine restrictions.

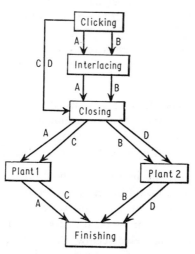

Fig. 33. Production flow chart

When we impose the set of parallel lines representing equal profits on this graph we can similarly find the point of maximum profitability. When we have two products and many machines we will find that in general only two machines will be working at their maximum capacity while all the others have spare capacity available when profit is being maximized. This is because it would be rare for the relative times that the different products take on the different machines to be so well in balance as to match completely with their relative profitability.

Let us now take a simple example which shows how one can state and deal with a more complex problem than the previous one, that is where there are more than 2 products. We now have a production line consisting of 6 different processes. Through these processes pass 8 products, 2 in each of 4 main categories, A, B, C and D. Not all categories go through the same processes and the way in which these products in the 4 categories are moved through the 7 processes is shown in Fig. 33 (page 87).

On 4 of the 6 processes there are restrictions in the total number of machine hours available for workings and these are—

>   Process 2—*Interlacing*: 2,400 machine hours
>   Process 3—*Closing*: 12,000 machine hours
>   Process 4—*Making plant 1*: 12,000 machine hours
>   Process 5—*Making plant 2*: 24,000 machine hours

To decide how much of each of the 8 products should be made in order to maximize the total contribution to profit we now ask what is the demand which each unit of the 8 end-products will impose on the processes through which they pass, and the table below shows the number of machine hours which is taken by the production of one unit of each of the 8 products.

Style	A_1	A_2	B_1	B_2	C_1	C_2	D_1	D_2
Interlacing	5	6	4	4	—	—	—	—
Closing	15	20	12	15	15	15	10	12
Plant 1	30	20	—	—	20	30	—	—
Plant 2	—	—	60	60	—	—	50	80

For example, reference to the flow chart (Fig. 33) shows that style A_1, which falls in the A category, will pass through processes clicking, interlacing, closing, making plant 1 and finishing. There is unlimited capacity on clicking and finishing and hence the only processes with capacity restriction through which style A_1 passes are interlacing, closing and making plant 1. The number of machine hours that 1 unit of style A_1 takes to go through each of these three processes is shown in the appropriate column of the table on page 88. This table is a quantification of the flow chart.

The information so far listed has been that stemming from production, namely the demands the products make and the capacities available to meet these demands. A third question has to be answered before the problem can be solved. This is the contribution to profit made by each of the 8 products. These are, in terms of the cash contribution (in £s) that one unit of each of these end-products will make, respectively

A_1	£5	C_1	£5
A_2	£5	C_2	£6
B_1	£4	D_1	£4
B_2	£4	D_2	£5

As can be seen, with more than two processes it is not possible to solve these problems by the graphical methods shown previously but the principle of the method of solution is the same. We know, from the basic logic, that the optimum solution will coincide with a product mix corresponding to at least one pair of points where the capacity restrictions meet. There is a finite number of such possible solutions and the techniques of linear programming are devised so as to travel successively around these possible alternatives until they discover the optimum. The mathematics of methods for solving these problems are given by Sasieni, Yaspan and Friedman.[1] The solution of the present problem would come out

[1] op. cit.

Production Constraints Only

Style	A₁	A₂	B₁	B₂	C₁	C₂	D₁	D₂	Capacity	Surplus non-critical restrictions	Bonus for relaxing critical restraint (per batch)
Contribution to profit	5	5	4	4	5	6	4	5			
Production — Interlacing	5	6	4	4					2,400	2,400	
Production — Closing Plant I	15	20	12	15	15	15	10	12	12,000		0·2
Production — Plant 2	30	20	60	60	20	30	50	80	12,000		0·1
									24,000		0·04
Solution (batches)					240	240	480				
Cost of introducing batch	1·0	1·0	0·8	1·4				0·6			

Total contribution to profit £4,550

as shown in the table on p. 90. As can be seen, the top left-hand half of this table presents the basic information on production and selling. The optimum solution shows that of the 8 products, only 3 are made, namely C_1, C_2 and D_1 with amounts of 240, 240 and 480 respectively. When this optimum solution is actually manufactured, the last two columns of the table show that 3 of the processes are critical, that is they will be working to capacity (the reader can check this by working out the production demands on the 4 processes resulting from the optimum solution). If each of these 3 processes in turn can be increased marginally in capacity there would clearly be a gain in total profit. The last column of the table shows that of the 3 processes, closing would give the greatest marginal increase in profitability, if a marginal increase in capacity could be obtained. Reference to the 2 product 3 machine cases discussed earlier will show that one has to be very careful in extrapolating marginal returns over major increases of capacity, the problem being that if one provides a great increase in capacity on one particular machine it may, in terms of the optimum solution, cease to be critical.

Returning to the above table one can see that when the optimum product maximum is produced the interlacing process is not used at all, since this process is divided into two categories A and B. The solution also gives one further piece of information. If any one of the 5 styles, which do not appear in the optimum solution, is forced into production, the cost of introducing it, measured in terms of the new optimum solution which will then be worked out taking account of this fresh restriction, is shown in the bottom row of the table on page 90. This gives some measure of the relative lack of desirability of the 5 products which do not form part of the optimum solution.

So far we have dealt with a production problem in which

Market Constraint Added

Style	A_1	A_2	B_1	B_2	C_1	C_2	D_1	D_2	Capacity	Surplus non-critical restrictions	Bonus for relaxing critical restraint (per batch)
Contribution to profit	5	6	4	4							
Production — Interlacing									2,400	1,580	0·17
Production — Closing Plant 1	15	20	12	15	15	15	10	12	12,000		0·08
Production — Closing Plant 2	30	20	60	60	20	30	50	80	24,000		0·05
Market . . . C					1	1			300		1·0
Solution (batches)	20	120			300	480					
Cost of introducing batch			0·8	1·3	0·17			0·73			

Total contributions £4,420

the only capacity restraints are those of the production plant. Marketing restraints can also be added. Suppose, for example, that the maximum total sales possible for all C category goods is 300. As can be seen, the above solution would have to be re-worked since it implies that the total production of C quality goods is 480. The table and solution would then be drawn up as in the table on p. 92.

The introduction of this market restraint causes a loss of contribution to profit of 140 and the products to be produced now total 4 including 1 from each of the 4 categories. It can be seen that the new market restraint is critical in the sense that the optimum solution produces right up to the restraint.

The Introduction of Probability

In the above examples we have assumed that what is produced will actually be sold, at a fixed contribution to profit. There will be cases where this is not so. For example when one is dealing with transient-life products one may be faced with the following type of example. We have a number of end-products, each of which is called a line, and for each of which there will be a seasonal life. The seasons for all the products may not coincide. In general, at the peak of a season the rate at which orders are being received is greater than the production capacity and sales must be made out of stock. In this situation there are two sorts of error into which we might fall. On the one hand we will manufacture goods which fail to be sold by the end of the season, and will then have to be sold at a distress selling price. On the other we may fail to make goods and so run out of stock and lose the profits which would have been yielded. Assuming that all the goods which we can make impose the same demand on the production processes, measured in the time needed to produce them, is it possible to review the finished goods stocks week by week so as always to be manufacturing those goods which have the greatest potential contribution to profits?

We do this by joining together two concepts, the first is the expected profitability of a line and the second is a derivation by a probability forecast of its ultimate season's sales.

By the expected probability we mean the conjunction of (*a*) the relative probabilities of a batch of goods either being sold or failing to be sold, and (*b*) the contribution to profits stemming from a sale at full price compared with the contribution stemming from a distress price. (This latter contribution may be negative, it does not affect the argument.)

For example, suppose that we were able to estimate that the probability is seventy per cent that a batch of a particular line put into production next week would be sold by the end of the season. There is therefore a probability of thirty per cent that it will not be sold. If the contribution to profit from the successful sale of the batch is £100, and the contribution to profit of making it and having to sell at a distress price at the end of the season is £10, then the expected profitability of making the batch is seventy per cent of £100+ thirty per cent of £10, that is £73. Hence, if week by week we could break down the potential production of all the lines which we could manufacture, into batches, and if for each batch we can estimate the probability that it will be sold, then we could fill up our manufacturing capacity with the particular batch of goods which maximizes our profits. We have, therefore, reduced the problem to one of making probability forecasts.

These probability forecasts can sometimes be presented as shown in Figs. 34 and 35.

Often there is a build-up of seasonal sales, of the type with which we are dealing, to a peak during the season and a typical relationship is as shown in these figures.

The graphs opposite may be typical for ranges of goods and

for these we can express the graph of the cumulative curve, as one where the maximum obtained at the end of the season is expressed as a hundred per cent point. It is a way of bringing all graphs to the same height (Fig. 36.)

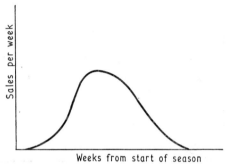

Fig. 34. *Average sales per week as season progresses*

Fig. 35. *Cumulative sales achieved during the season*

A relationship of this sort derived historically may show, for example, that after five weeks of the season, ten per cent of the ultimate season's sales will *on average* have been made. Naturally when we take individual items historically, we should not find that in all cases five weeks corresponded to the ten per cent point. Sometimes it would be less, sometimes more, but the average would be the ten per cent figure. We might find, for example, that the ratio of total season's sales to the five-week figure was distributed as in Fig. 37.

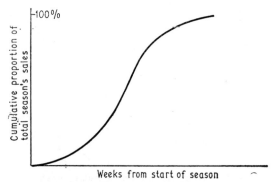

Fig. 36. Cumulative proportion of season's sales

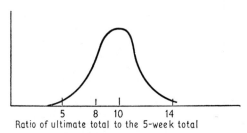

Fig. 37. Statistical distribution of total season's sales to the achievement after 5 weeks

The use of this graph provides us with a way of obtaining a probability estimate that a particular batch will be sold. Let us put some numbers into an example.

Suppose that after five weeks we have sold 1,000 batches of a particular line and have manufactured a total of 8,000 batches. The probability that, if we manufacture 100 more batches next week these will be sold by the end of the season is the probability that the total season's sales will exceed 8,100 batches. This is gained from Fig. 37, as being the probability that the ratio of total season's sales to the five-week figure will actually exceed 8·1. This can be derived from the graph as being the proportion of the area under it to the right of 8·1, say 90 per cent. If the two profitability figures of selling and failing to sell are £100 and £10 per batch then the expected contribution of manufacturing 100 batches of this particular line will be $0.90 \times 100 + 0.10 \times 10 = £91$. If we make this same calculation for each of the alternative lines which can be manufactured, we could determine that particular line for which the expected contribution to profit is maximized. The first production decision therefore, is to allocate resources to produce 100 batches of this particular line and the next decision is whether we should manufacture a second 100 batches of this line or whether it should be 100 of another line. It is clear that the expected profitability of the second 100, which would evolve a lower probability of being sold out of the first 100, would be lower than the first 100. In this way, batch by batch, the total production capacity is filled up for the coming week so as to maximize the total expected contribution to profits.

The linear programming approaches as outlined earlier in this chapter are of great importance in large industries, such as oil, where the mathematical development has been pioneered. It is tempting to regard problems of allocation as being synonymous with mathematical devices. This is probably true in those problems where full unidimensional measures of input, output and objective are available. In others we are straining to derive valid measures.

The allocation of resources in a hospital depends on our being able to derive measures of the effort being applied to various categories of illness and, more important, to measures of patient *need*. In the fight against crime, we are still groping for measures of the cost and the effectiveness of different parts of the police force, for "effectiveness" implies that we know clearly what a police force is supposed to be optimizing. In the allocation of effort into the different research projects carried out in a research establishment we are groping for measures of the probability that a particular project will succeed within a stated time period. It is in these new areas of allocation that the really exciting work is going on, rather than in the elegant mathematical dances which form the basic bread and butter allocation problems.

VI

HUMAN PROBLEMS

IT will be noticed that, although so far, we have been dealing with problems involving the basic components of decision making namely men, machines, money, materials and markets, and, although in all the models which have been discussed, man may appear implicitly, it is still true that it has always been assumed that all men are equal and are equally unimportant. This reflects the development of operational research. For the research scientist has always been coy about studying the problems of man and his environment. One of the reasons for this has been that we were very conscious that the social scientist was already heavily involved in these problems; we were also aware of the complex, even indeterminate nature of the problems and we have tended to concentrate on well structured, concrete areas, such as production. Now it is clear from the earlier chapters that there is no such thing as an operational research problem. There are only problems. All the specialists who are interested in management problems, whether they be economists, engineers, operational research workers or social scientists, look at these problems in different ways. The difference then is one of approach and is not between the problems themselves. There is, of course, a subjective element in the approach to problems. Although perhaps, the problem exists uniquely in the absolute, once any of us from the background of our expertise or of our history surveys a management problem it is immediately seen in a subjective form. Many scientists fail to see this. They assume that these problems exist absolutely and uniquely in the way in which they are seen by the research worker himself. Many of the standard textbooks on the subject assume that the vision of the problem as seen by the research worker is unique and is absolute. It is perhaps a weakness of the operational research approach that we do not have the same problem studied by different groups of research workers in the same situation, so that we may compare the variety of approaches to model building that a group of operational research workers would display among themselves.

In this chapter we shall survey some of the approaches of the operational research worker to the study of groups of people and their influence on the objectives of organizations. The first of these studies will be concerned with the people themselves and their reaction to their environment, and stems from some work carried out by the operational research group of the National Coal Board a few years ago.[1]

This was a study of the factors influencing the wastage of miners from the collieries. It is necessary during a programme of changing the pattern of employment in an industry, in which in some areas there is going to be a phased decline in the number of men employed, while in other areas there is going to be an increase in the labour force, to know what are the factors which cause people to leave their employment. This is particularly essential in coal mining, as the costs of training replacement labour are very high, of the order of £1,000 per man.

When the O.R. team was asked to study this problem the first step was to visit a number of "typical" collieries in the British coal-fields. What one means by typical is not very clear but certainly one would have to study collieries in highly urban as well as rural areas, large collieries as well as small, and highly mechanized ones as well as those with the older

[1] HOULDEN, B. T., Operational Research and its Application in the United Kingdom Coal Industry, The Mining Engineer No. 18, March, 1962.

type of hand-worked faces. A large amount of data covering mine workers' leaving collieries was examined. These data gave information about coal miners who left the pits, but it was also necessary to study coal miners who stayed. In terms of the time factor, two features emerged as important. In

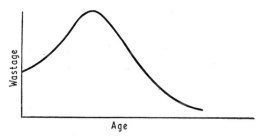

Fig. 38. The relationship between age and labour wastage

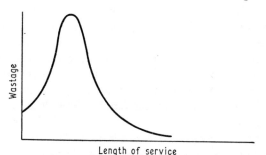

Fig. 39. The relationship between length of service and wastage

Figs. 38 and 39 we see that of every 100 coal miners starting work at a given age, the length of service until they left the colliery which was employing them has a very high peak in the early years of service. This corresponded also with a peak age for leaving coal mines.

Since most men are recruited to the mines in their late teens, the age at which they leave will be correlated with the number of years they have served when they leave. Obviously too, the age at which they leave corresponds with a marrying age. On marriage the young man will be pressed by his wife to leave what is a rather dirty shift industry and get a clean-collar job in a neighbouring factory, if this is available. There is an additional statistical quirk. When a mine worker leaves one colliery and transfers to another because he has moved to live near his wife's parents, his leaving is recorded as a loss of a man. Hence some of this peaking of leaving the industry at the age of 22 is false, and is merely one side of a transfer from one colliery to another. Nevertheless there is a significant feature involved in this length of service.

It might be interesting in passing to reflect on the implications of these results in areas outside the mining industry. The implication is that if we are seeking to increase a labour force (or indeed a management or research force since there is nothing necessarily unique to labour in these results) we must be prepared to see the rate of turnover of staff increase markedly. In many organizations one takes the loss rate of staff as being a measure of employee morale and, particularly for management and scientific research staff, it is felt to be disastrous when this turnover rate increases. It is not often that this rate as such is presented in more realistic terms than as a straight percentage loss per year. Sometimes senior management is disturbed to see, in an expanding industry where there is a great demand for more staff and top manage-ment believes that employees at all levels will feel that the opportunities for a career in the organization are markedly improved, just at this time a significant increase of the loss of staff. This in fact is not, in a period of increase in staff, an indication of lowering of morale. Turnover figure may be used as a valid measure of employee morale in times of stability, but in times of rapid increase of staff one must expect as a corollary that the turnover rate will increase.

This imposes an additional problem for the organization since loss of staff does tend to be contagious. Once a few people leave an organization, the others who are left get concerned lest those who are leaving have perceived some dark cloud on the horizon or some rock in the sea that those who are staying on the ship have failed to observe. Those remaining tend to put on their life-jackets and jump into the water fairly rapidly. Hence any period of increase of employee force, of whatever nature whether technical or administrative, or labour, must be expected to produce by itself an increase, perhaps highly significant in staff turnover. At the same time it can be seen that if in an organization we want to increase staff by perhaps one hundred people, then we may have to budget for recruiting and training perhaps three or four hundred people in order to achieve the new level of stable employee force at the increased numbers.

It was in fact this latter point which now occupied the minds of the research workers. They could see that there were time- and age-dependent factors influencing loss of mine workers. They could also see that in areas where an increase of labour was needed, the costs of training this labour would be much higher than normally budgeted. The industry was not faced with simply the cost of £1,000 for every extra man needed but a larger factor than this, because the number of those needed to be recruited would be far more than the difference between the new labour force and the old. It could also be calculated that it would take three years for the turnover rate to stabilize. This led, as an extension of the work, to investigating what other factors there were which were affecting the loss of labour and also the possibility of its recruitment. It was shown that the physical features of the colliery were less important than its geographical situation relative to potential manpower. The manpower catchment map for the area around the collieries was taken and on these maps were plotted, from the colliery records, the points where the mine workers were living. The research team could also plot on these maps the mine workers who had left the colliery during the past year. When this was done a very interesting feature emerged—not only was it shown that the longer the distance the man had to travel to work the greater was the chance that he would leave work during the year, but also that this fall-off was very rapid in terms of travelling time. This can be seen better in the form of the graph in Fig. 40.

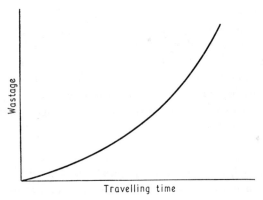

Fig. 40. The relationship between travelling time and wastage

Very approximately, if the travelling time of one group of men to work compared with another is doubled, then the loss rate per year in the group that travels the further distance will be also doubled. Where the comparable travelling time from one group to another is three times as great, then the loss rate will be three times as much. There is a square law which seems to relate the loss rate to work with the travelling time for distances of more than three miles. This led the team immediately to look at the probability of recruiting labour. A map of an area was taken and concentric circles were drawn on it, where the radius of the circle represented travelling time to the colliery. The labour supply as a percentage of the population approximately decreased as the square of the radius of the circle involved. There was therefore an effect present, for both recruitment and wastage of labour, in which travelling distance was important in a dominant fashion. An obvious move now was to lay on special bus services to take workers to and from the collieries, since anything which reduced travelling time would not only reduce wastage but also increase the probability of labour recruitment.

Typical results would show that for a colliery in a rural area, annual wastage is low for workers living within two miles and so if an adequate supply is available within this radius then it will be possible to have a labour force with high stability, for example less than ten per cent annual wastage. If, however, there is little supply of labour within, say, five miles the loss rate will be serious.

It could also be shown that if, in order to expand its labour force, a colliery should recruit men from beyond ten miles, the situation then becomes insupportable. The research found that it was cheaper for the National Coal Board to build houses for rent to accommodate experienced mine workers close to their places of employment, even though the cost per worker, over and above rent received, was £45 per year.

There is one interesting point: as has been said, the dominant feature in attracting men to a colliery is the distance of travel to work and there is a square law associated with this, and so we have a simple equation of the form $A \times \dfrac{K}{R^2}$, where A is a parameter associated with the colliery, K is a constant and R is the travelling time to work. Further study of the factor K showed that two other features influenced it. One was that in regions of high unemployment, the fall-off of attraction of a colliery, measured in terms of the possibility of recruiting labour to it, was much slower than in regions of low unemployment. Hence we have a new form of this simple recruitment model, namely $A = K \times \dfrac{E}{R^2}$, where E is now the level of unemployment.

We now recall the law of magnetic attraction, that is the attractiveness of a magnet in a magnetic field varies proportionately to the pole strength of the magnet, m, the conductivity of the field, e, and the square of the distance of the point to the pole, d, that is $A = \dfrac{m \times e}{d^2}$.

One should not make too much of this similarity, but it is remarkable that a study of the attractiveness of coal mines to coal miners should come to the same answer as the study of the attractiveness of a magnet to an iron filing on a magnetic field.

For an account of this work see Houlden.[1]

What of Morale?

In many industries there have been studies of loosely related factors such as accidents, absenteeism, labour wastage, and industrial disputes, all of which may be looked on in some way as symptoms of morale effect. There is a story that some years ago a research team in the steel industry had been studying the make-up of various morale factors and had seen, in a number of steel-works, the way in which these four features either increased or decreased together. On visiting another steel company as part of this investigation they observed from the data that whereas the accident rate, absenteeism and labour wastage were all high, the rate of industrial disputes, measured in man-hours lost by strikes per

[1] op. cit.

year, was much lower than average. In a light-hearted aside to the managing director they remarked that this steel mill must be about due for a major strike. Curiously, a few weeks later the complete works was stopped, by a major dispute. The reputation of the team was made in this particular plant, although one shudders to think what the odds were against this actually occurring so quickly.

Some of the most interesting work in this field has been carried out by Revans.[1] His original work in this field was in the mining industry where he carried out studies of morale as evidenced by these four major factors. One finding in Revans's work in the mining industry was the importance of communication as a determinant in morale. Revans has extended his work into studies of hospitals and the communication pattern within them. This work is extremely interesting. What one is trying to do here is to see not only the influence of communication on morale, but how to define communication and the relationship of the pattern of communication within a hospital on the productivity. This means then that one has to try to define productivity as such.

The measurements of productivity of hospitals are of course extremely important in terms of the allocation of national effort and expenditure between different hospitals. The Ministry of Health at one time used the percentage bed occupancy as a measure of the load imposed on a hospital. Since consultants will be reluctant to discharge a patient from hospital unless there is another patient ready to take his place patient stay was influenced by a government statistic.

Another measure of productivity which has been applied to hospitals is the rate at which patients are discharged from the hospital. At first sight it seems perfectly acceptable until one realizes that this rate of discharge implies alive or dead.

[1] REVANS, R. G., Hospital Attitudes and Communication, in *Operational Research and the Social Sciences*, Ed. J. Lawrence (Wiley).

In these terms the most productive hospital would be one in which every patient admitted died within twenty-four hours.

Studies of this type of service industry are not easy. They are not easy because of the difficulty of defining objectives, of deciding, for example, what one has achieved by treating a certain patient in a certain way; of deciding whether it is better to treat more patients who have minor ailments compared with a relatively few who have serious ones. There is again the constant difficulty of relating cost to return and the emotional block which one meets if one tries to carry out some form of cost effectiveness in a hospital. It is sometimes felt to be wrong and unethical to compare the money expended per cancer patient with say the money expended per patient admitted for a hysterectomy.

The original approach of Revans to these problems was to try to measure something which is relevant. Measures of patient stay for different classes of condition in different sorts of hospital showed some startling differences. It was found for example that hospitals where appendectomies or hernia repairs are discharged sooner than average also tend to discharge their cardiacs and diabetics sooner. Some of this is shown in the table opposite which covers five hospitals in the north-west of England.

Clearly one needs information on the condition of patients on admission and on their history subsequent to discharge. For patients from one hospital, say 5, may well not impose any further strain on the G.P. service on discharge because they are discharged in a better condition of health than those patients from hospital 1 who stay for a shorter time. Nevertheless there does seem to be a significance and Revans's next point was to see what other factors about these hospitals were correlated with the patients' stay, for by implication one now is saying that hospital 1 is a more highly productive hospital than hospital 5.

Rank Orders of Patient Stay at Five Hospitals

Hospital	Diagnostic class				
	i	ii	iii	iv	v
I	I	I	2	I	I
2	2	2	3	3	2
3	3	3	I	2	3
4	4	4	4	5	4
5	5	5	5	4	5

(i) Appendectomy, (ii) Hernia repair, (iii) Partial gastrectomy, (iv) Cholecystectomy, (v) Respiratory

Two interesting points emerged from this investigation. The first was the rate of turnover of the nurses. When these five hospitals were ranked in order of the rate at which nurses were lost both during training and subsequent to full training it was found that the hospitals where patients stayed longer were also the hospitals with the higher rate of turnover of nurses.

Rank Order of Average Length of Stay of Different Hospital Staff for the Same Five Hospitals

Hospital	i	ii	iii	iv	v	vi
I	I	2	2	I	$1\frac{1}{2}$	I
2	4	I	I	2	$4\frac{1}{2}$	2
3	2	3	3	4	$1\frac{1}{2}$	3
4	5	5	4	5	3	4
5	3	4	5	3	$4\frac{1}{2}$	5

(i) Matrons and deputy matrons (iv) Assistant nurses
(ii) Sisters   (v) Domestics
(iii) Staff nurses   (vi) Student nurses

In fact, if we take the loss rate of nurses from a hospital as being a measure of the morale of the nursing staff, we find that low morale is associated with low productivity and high morale with high productivity. It is not at this stage sufficient to say that productivity is low because morale is low, rather than vice versa, and indeed these definitions or descriptions of morale and productivity are both open to discussion. But the third point which this research discovered was a feature of the communication pattern within these hospitals.

Research students were placed in the wards and at random intervals of time they observed what the student nurses, staff nurses, sisters and matrons were doing. One of the factors which they observed was the number of times when a staff nurse was talking to a sister or a sister talking to the matron, and so on. Again, startling differences emerged in the pattern between different hospitals. In some hospitals there was a very high degree of discussion among the nursing staff, in others there was almost none. The reader by now will not be surprised to learn that when the hospitals were ranked in order of the amount of discussion within the nursing staff the rank order was very similar to that of productivity and of turnover, namely hospitals with a high degree of discussion and conversation between the nursing staff were hospitals with a low turnover rate of nursing staff and with a low patient stay.

Private conversations were also held with the nursing staff on their general attitudes to each other. Nurses were asked whether they found the sister overbearing, helpful, rude, polite, condescending and so on. Sisters were asked complementary questions about their nurses and the attitudes of sisters and the matron to each other were also discussed. The results of these studies showed also that the attitudes of staff to each other were very closely conditioned by the amount of discussion. Again it is difficult to tell which is the chicken and which is the egg, but it is becoming clear from these studies that there may well be an important link between the communication pattern, the opportunities of staff to discuss problems with each other, and morale and productivity.

Some Laboratory Experiments

Some of these conclusions are supported, but not completely, by laboratory experiments which have been carried out in a number of American universities. The classic work in this field was some studies carried out by Bavelas some years ago in the Massachusetts Institute of Technology. Bavelas took groups of students and set them problems to solve. All of these problems were of the nature where the team was given a job to do and information was divided among the members of the team. Different teams had different communication patterns imposed on them. Some of these are shown in Fig. 41.

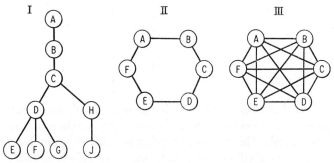

Fig. 41. Different communication patterns imposed on a task team

The interest was to see what the effect of the communication pattern imposed on the team was on the rate at which they were able to perform the tasks set them. It was found that the more hierarchical communication patterns were more efficient in terms of the reduction of time needed to solve the tasks. Hence, of those communication patterns shown, a dictatorial pattern such as I undoubtedly was the best in terms of problem-solving time. On the other hand when the teams were asked which patterns they enjoyed most. the completely democratic, or even anarchic, pattern III was the one they chose. This was, unfortunately, the most in-efficient in terms of time taken to solve the problems. One very interesting point however did emerge from these studies. This was that when the performance of individual members of the team was evaluated, it was seen that irrespective of his natural ability, a man who was at the centre of a communication network emerged as a man of authority in the problem-solving task. If we look at the different positions in the structure I we can classify each of them in the following way in terms of the number of communication channels which come into or out of each of these positions.

Structure I	Channels Available
A	1
B	2
C	3
D	4
E	1
F	1
G	1
H	2
J	1

As can be seen, position D is the most dominant in this structure and a man at D would tend to dominate the problem-solving task. This has an interesting parallel within industry and in organization structure in industry. This is certainly reflected by the author's own experience in the mining industry a few years ago.[1]

At that time he was studying the use of underground communication systems in coal mines (to which reference will be made in Chapter VIII). This required research teams to sit at telephone switchboards, generally underground at collieries, and to log all calls made through the system. All of these calls are connected with the managing of the colliery, both for routine coal production, and for dealing with special

[1] CLAPHAM, J. C. R. and DUNN, H. D., Underground Communications, Proc. First Inter. Conf. on OR., 1957 (E.U.P.).

emergencies such as the breakdown of a piece of loading equipment, the failure of a trunk conveyor belt, or the shortage of empty trucks at an underground loading point where coal is loaded from a conveyor belt on to an underground train. As part of his duties the telephone operator at a colliery will listen in to all calls made in the pit. Consequently he knows far more about what is going on than does the manager or any of the other members of the staff. Hence if a loading point is running out of empty tubs he will hear the loading point operator exclaim that he is running out of trucks. The operator himself will then contact another loading point and have trucks sent across to the point with shortage. If there is a breakdown of a face conveyor belt, which then stops the whole coal face working, the operator will hear the face foreman on the phone asking for the fitter. The telephone operator will know where the fitter is because a short while ago he will have heard him on the phone in another part of the colliery. He can track him down. So the telephone operator, who is often selected by the random process of his being a man who has suffered an injury, emerges in a position of great power in a coal mine and tends to run the pit in the absence, or even in the presence, of the manager. This is a remarkable parallel with Bavelas's experiments.

This has also a parallel in industrial management. One of the features of industry in recent years has been the emergence of the accountant in a position of power within the organization. Of all disciplines, accounting is probably the one which is most frequently represented on boards of companies. Engineering companies may not have a professional engineer on the board of directors but will almost certainly have an accountant. The accountant has emerged in his position of power, probably because he is at the centre of a communication network. In all organizations accounting is the last function to be decentralized, for the control over finance, expenditure, and income is one which is retained at the centre of organizations. Hence the accountant is a man who is at the centre of a very well defined communication network, and almost inevitably emerges in a position of authority in the organization. It is interesting, in passing, to reflect on the likely change which large-scale automatic data processing is going to make. For this is going to demand technical skills which the accountant does not necessarily possess. He is going to be fed with information from a channel which he does not control, and this information is going to be the same as that received by all other members of the management team. We may therefore now have seen the accountant reach his peak of influence and we may well now see the electronic data processer, particularly if he is the sort of man who is concerned with the well-being of his company rather than of his computer, emerge into a position of significant authority in company organizations.

When one seeks to study the behaviour of people one is always told that the individual is unpredictable and we cannot forecast what a man is going to do. We are then invited to draw the conclusion that since we cannot forecast the behaviour of an individual (and this is questionable), we certainly cannot forecast the behaviour of groups. It is implied that in magnifying from the individual to the group we are magnifying the difficulty of forecasting, but we are, in fact, minimizing it. To take an analogy, consider a kettle of boiling water. We know from the principles of physics that at a given pressure water will boil at 100°C. We also know, in terms of the rate at which heat is being applied to the base of the kettle, the rate at which molecules of water will be transformed into molecules of steam. We know then, the behaviour of water in the mass in terms of its transformation into steam in the mass. But we do not know, from even so exact a science as physics, which will be the next molecule of water to be transformed. This is quite indeterminate, but if we are faced with this fundamental indeterminacy, we do not need to say that we cannot tell the rate at which molecules of water will be turned into molecules of steam, even though we cannot select the next one to be transformed. In the same way an insurance company cannot tell which of its policy holders will die in the next calendar year, but the whole basis of insurance is formulated on the hypothesis that they can forecast very accurately how many will die.

The behaviour of the group then is much more easy to deal with than the behaviour of the individual, and in so far as we are concerned with the attitudes and reactions of groups with their environment then it is possible by measurement to be of assistance to management. These studies show the importance of trying to derive fundamental measures that are relevant in the situation involved. Clearly in much of this work we are still groping for first measures, but measurement, sorting and classification are basic to all science and are nothing to be ashamed of.

VII

THE COMPETITIVE PROBLEM

So far in the chapters of this book we have attempted to show both the way in which different types of problem can be formulated with a structure associated with them, and the way in which the methods of scientific research can be deployed so as to build the model appropriate to the particular kind of problem being studied.

As can be seen from these studies the decision maker has essentially been dealing with basic models of the form $E = f(x_1, x_2, \ldots x_n, y_1, y_2, \ldots y_m)$, where the x's are the factors which the decision maker has under his direct control, and the y's are the factors which he cannot control, but which he has to take into account when deciding on an optimum strategy.

Implicit in all these models has been the assumption that the y's will not react against the decision maker in terms of the controllable x's which are selected by him. The decision maker therefore is faced with a non-reactive situation. This is often called playing a game against nature.

Clearly the problems of business decision making in which one is considering the best strategy to apply against an opponent may well not fall into this category, for each opponent will also be able to observe what the other is doing and will derive strategies in terms of his own objective. Consequently the outcome of the decision is the result of a joint action by two or more competitors and the approach to these problems is of a markedly different kind from those in which the decision maker is only trying to deal with a non-malevolent environment such as nature.

Notwithstanding this, there are some problems of competition in which because of a sluggishness in reaction from the opponent, the situation may be treated as a game against nature. The strictly competitive problem is one in which there is a very quick reaction from an opponent; indeed it may be of a special kind which we shall discuss later, in which the outcome of a decision can only be made manifest when an opponent has also made a decision. There is in problems of this type a mating of two or more opponents and a progeny of outcomes.

But let us consider first a specific problem of the type which, while containing a competitive element, because of the sluggish response of an opponent can be regarded as a game against nature. The type of problem we shall consider is one of a family called bidding problems. In these problems a number of competitors seek to formulate a strategy separately, in terms of which the objective will be shared between the bidders, in a way which depends on the strategies which they have adopted. If bidders' behaviour remains homogeneous over a period of time, then it is possible for one of the competitors to look on all his opponents as being purely nature and to derive a competitive strategy which will optimize his own performance.

To do this depends on being able to identify the characteristics in an opponent's behaviour which are constant and also to identify those other characters which depend in specific ways on specific factors which can be delineated in any practical situation. Let us consider a definite example. One type of bidding problem arises in the United States oil industry where periodically pieces of land, which are thought to be oil-bearing, are placed on the market. Competitors are allowed to inspect these pieces of land and to submit sealed bids for the rights. On a given day all these bids are declared and the highest bidder on each piece of land is awarded it. The problem as initially posed by an oil company was, given an amount of money which they had to spread out on bids and given the characteristic of the land offered in a sale, in terms of potential oil yields, how should the money be spread out in bids among these pieces of land so as to maximize the expected return to the company?

One difficulty facing researchers in this type of problem is that the value of a piece of land is potential rather than actual. It is not possible to forecast, more than approximately, the oil yield of a piece of land. One device which is commonly adopted is for the geologists to survey all the pieces of land on offer, and to assign to each one an arbitrary index number on a scale from 0 to 100 which assesses its potential oil yield (increase of index number indicates an increasing potential oil yield).

Often in these situations one has to adopt or work towards a strategy for a company which, rather than strictly maximizing the oil yield will, instead, maximize the total number of index points which the company wins. This begs a number of questions. It assumes, in particular, that these indices are additive. That is, for example, a piece of land with an index of 40 and another with an index of 50, would be equally desirable compared with two other pieces of land with indices of 20 and 70. This forms an interesting illustration of the way in which the research worker may have to build assumptions into his model, and he must be careful to be quite explicit when presenting the results of his research and to make clear what these assumptions will mean in practice.

In the particular case study which is the subject of this example, the research team spent some time working through the historical data. Some of these data were well documented for, since the sales are matters of concern to the States involved, good records must be kept, over a long period of time, of the actual bids submitted by different companies on each of the tracts which have been put up for sale.

In a particular sale up to one hundred tracts may be offered and perhaps up to ten companies will bid on each one of these. The team attempted to see what factors there were that influenced the size of bids made. It was difficult to do this because, although the sizes of the bids were known, there was great difficulty in working through the companies' records and obtaining the indices (called the "X value") which the geologists had assigned to tracts of land which had been the subject of sales in the past. Eventually however most of these indices were determined, and the research was then aimed at

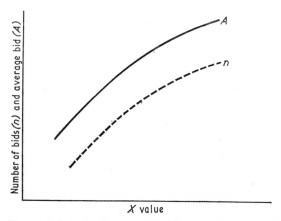

Fig. 42. *Relationship between potential value and the number of bids and the average bid*

trying to see what features affected the bids of the competition. In this, a number of interesting features emerged. It was noted that when tracts were on offer for which the company's own geologists had assigned high index figures, then the number of bids made by the competition was increased and the average of these bids was also increased. On the other hand when the companies' geologists had

assigned low index values to pieces of land, not many companies were interested enough to put in bids, and the bids
that they put in were on the average lower. These two statements can be shown graphically as in Fig. 42.

It is always necessary when graphs of this form are presented to inquire into the variability about the relationship
plotted. There was indeed significant variability about the
relationship but nevertheless the trend gave good indications
of the potential number of competitors and their average bids.

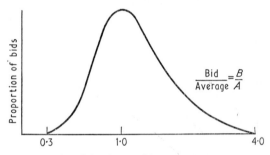

Fig. 43. Statistical distribution of the ratio of bid to the average

Although all this was interesting and showed that the team
were on the right track, it was not sufficient to draw up a
bidding strategy. What was still lacking was any forecast of
the variability of rival bids about the average. A large number
of attempts were made to determine methods of estimating
this method of variability, and eventually one method did
seem to offer outstanding advantages. When the team studied
the relationship of bids submitted for particular tracts in the
past to the average of the bids made on the tract in question,
they saw emerge a relationship which is shown in Fig. 43.

From this it can be seen that there is a family relationship.
When we take the ratio $\frac{B}{A}$, there is a peaking of occurrence

around 1, which is what we would expect, and there is very little chance of bids as high as three times the average or bids as low as one-third of the average being submitted. Hence if we can estimate, as we now can, the average of the rivals'

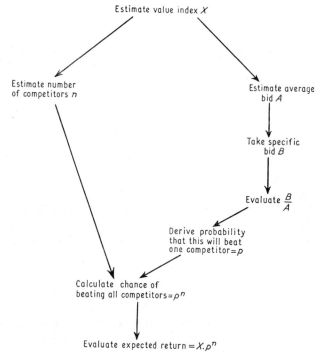

Fig. 44. The build-up of the probability of a bid winning and the expected return for a bid of a given size

bid we can also from this second relationship estimate the probability of a bid of any multiple of this average actually being submitted.

This led the research into deriving a strategy for bidding. First of all from the geologists' estimates of the value indices of the different tracts which had been submitted for sale, it was possible to estimate the average of the rival bids and their number. One could now take any specific bid which one could consider submitting on a specific piece of land, and, by relating it to the estimated average, work out the probability that this bid would beat one competitor, for this probability is represented by the proportion of the area of the relationship in Fig. 43 to the left of the value of $\dfrac{B}{A}$ in question. This probability of beating one rival bidder can be translated into the probability of this bid being an actual winning bid by raising the probability to the power of the number of rival bidders. We can describe this procedure in flow chart form (Fig. 44).

Let us take a specific example. Suppose on a tract with a value index of 60, the estimated number of rival bidders is 5 and their estimated average bid is $100,000. If we are considering submitting a bid of $200,000, the probability of this bid beating one rival bidder is represented by the area under the curve of Fig. 43 above lying to the left of the point $\dfrac{200,000}{100,000} = 2$. Suppose this probability is eighty-five per cent. This means that this bid has an eighty-five per cent chance of beating one rival. Hence, if we have a 0·85 chance of beating one rival bidder, the chance that we shall win, given our estimate that there will be 5 rival bidders, is 0·85 raised to the power of 5, that is

$$(0·85) \times (0·85) \times (0·85) \times (0·85) \times (0·85) = 0·44.$$

In this way we can for a given tract of land show graphically the relationship between a size of bid on this tract and the expected return. What we have to do is to take this relationship, which will be different for every one, for each of the tracts and show how a total bid can be divided into separate ones to maximize the total expected return. As can be seen we have now eliminated probability from the problem and are working in expected values; we have therefore transformed what was a competitive problem into an allocation problem, and this is the sort of problem which can be dealt with by the methods indicated in Chapter V.

A number of question marks can be placed against this example. First of all, we notice that the objective stated is a curious one. The objective is stated so as to maximize the return of index values in terms of a bid of a given amount. In practice one is not concerned about the amount bid but rather the amount which has to be paid out in winning bids. The team discussed this point with the oil company, but the company felt that as they were having to pledge their credit on bids, they were unwilling to go beyond the maximum amount they could pledge, irrespective of the likelihood of the amount they actually have to pay out in winning bids. One still feels this was unreal but it was their statement of their own objective function. The second point stems from the fact that this method can be shown to be optimal in the long run, that is for a given amount spread out on bids it will maximize the total index values returned in the end. For, as Keynes said in another context, in the long run we are all dead. Applied to the affairs of this particular company, this means that unless they get back a certain minimum amount of oil out of every sale, their sources of raw material will be exhausted and they will be in a very difficult situation. Hence it is necessary to amend the solution so as to ensure that there is a very high probability that a certain minimum amount of oil will be gained at each sale.

The model then is of the form—

$$E = f(x_1, x_2, x_3, \ldots x_n; B; X_1, X_2, \ldots, X_n;$$
$$\gamma_1, \gamma_2, \gamma_3, \ldots \gamma_m)$$

where

    E = expected total amount of X's won,

    Controllable variables—

      $x_1, x_2, \ldots x_3$ are the company's own bids

    Uncontrollable variables—

      B, the total amount bid

      $X_1, X_2, \ldots X_n$; are the value indices

      $y_1, y_2, \ldots y_m$ are rival bids

We notice that we treat B as being uncontrollable. Strictly one should derive E in terms of different values of B, but this the company were unwilling to do.

As we remarked at the beginning of this example, the solution is proposed in terms of a sluggish reaction from the competition. What happens when the competition realizes that one particular company is gaining far more than it has done in the past and is obviously using some new method of solution? Curiously enough this happened to the particular company which forms the subject of this study. Some time after the original study was carried out, a number of the geologists who were concerned in the study moved to other oil companies. One can ask the question, what does one do now, if one knows the method that the rival companies are going to use? We know the geologists assessing the value of tracts in different companies tend to behave in roughly the same sort of way. One can then evaluate what bids the rival companies are likely to submit in terms of the total amount which they are willing to bid. Assuming they are going to use this method, the strategy now would be not to work out one's own bids, for this would be pointless, but to estimate the bids of the rivals, then to work out one's own strategy knowing what the competition is going to do! Once the competition finds that, even though they are using a new method, they are not getting the return they expected, they will know that we know. We now have to derive a strategy in terms of what we know, that they know that we know. One can see a hierarchy of knowledge evolving and in this situation there would be a steady state of bids and of return from these bids, and one would be in a gaming situation of the type which we shall discuss later in this chapter. In fact, this possible line of development illustrates the essential transience of O.R. solutions, to which we refer in Chapter IX.

One can observe in this example the transition from one structure to another. If we are assuming a sluggish response, then the game against nature results. The probabilities are transformed into expected returns and we now find the structure of an allocation problem, for we are allocating a total amount bid, into bids on separate tracts, so as to maximize a yield. If the relationship between the announced bid on a tract, B, and the yield, X, was linear then we would have a problem that could be solved by linear programming of a simple form. But this is not so.

Once we start to allow a response by our competitors we move away from the structure of an allocation form into the direct gaming situation.

Of a similar type to this form of study are those investigations carried out in advertising and marketing. In these the assumption is still made that the response of a competitor will be sluggish. Sluggish, of course, is a relative term and by it we mean that there is a sequence of steps in which we take a decision, the competitor replies and then we take another decision and so on. Thus we are not in the situation described before in which the outcome can only be seen when both sides have made a decision.

Many attempts have been made in the field of advertising to try to derive methods which can estimate the amount of sales a product will gain in terms of the type and amount of the advertising to which it is subjected. Many difficulties underlie any historical analysis which relates sales to advertising

Obviously it is difficult, in terms of one particular company's activity, to try and derive estimates based on historical analysis of the company's activity alone because competitor's advertising affects the market. This means that

Year	Sales (£)	Advertising (10% of last years' sales)
1	1,000,000	—
2	1,200,000	100,000
3	1,300,000	120,000
4	1,500,000	130,000
5	1,400,000	150,000
6	1,300,000	140,000
7	1,100,000	130,000
8	800,000	110,000
9	900,000	80,000
10	1,000,000	90,000

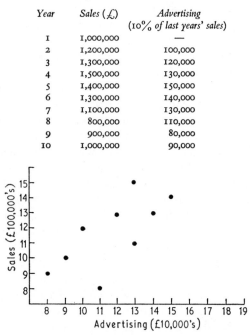

Fig. 45. The spurious relationship between sales and advertising when current advertising is set in terms of previous sales

controlled experiments cannot be carried out. In addition in many companies the amount of the advertising budget in any year is taken as a function of the sales achieved in the past year and hence we may find as shown in Fig. 45 and its accompanying table that we have forced a relationship of advertising to sales. For suppose we set our advertising budget so that this year we spend £10 on advertising for every £100 received in sales last year; let there be *no* causal relationship between advertising and sales and let the set of sales figures year by year be as given in the table accompanying Fig. 45. Advertising expenditure is not the independent variable which affects sales, but rather sales is the independent variable which affects advertising.

Some research workers have made inroads into the general problem. We are very far from getting any standard solution, and in fact anyone who proclaims that he has a complete solution to this particular type of problem should be looked on with some degree of suspicion.

One ingenious method which has been derived by M. G. Moroney is to relate share of advertising and share of market to each other. Moroney takes as two basic variables, a share of advertising, period by period and compares this with a product's share of market, period by period. He has evolved a working model of the following form—

$$S_{K+1} = aS_K + b(a_{K+1} - a_K)$$

where the factors are—

S_{K+1} = Share of market in this period (the $(K+1)$th)
S_K = Share of market in last period (the Kth)
a_{K+1} = Share of advertising this period
a_K = Share of advertising last period

In some researches this has shown interesting relationships, but it is still some way from perfection. As can be seen, this approach takes the present position, measured in terms of sales volume of the specified product and all rival products, as the base point. It then takes what is thought to be a relevant causal variable and the method relates *changes* in the causal variable to *changes* in the sales. There are forms of algebra which are well suited to this type of problem and difference equations and Markov processes have all been utilized to deal with these problems of *switching*.

Other workers have taken an estimated saturation market for a product and have evolved the concept of a net accumulated weight of advertising at any time. This net accumulated weight is a form of discounting past advertising, in terms of how far in the past it took place, and so to relate a stream of past advertising to an actual parameter as of today, which is called the net accumulated weight. It is then possible to use historical data to show the effect of weight of advertising on a share of market figure. These models take account of the

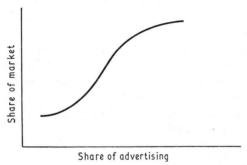

Fig. 46. The relationship between advertising effort and marketing achievement

fact that the nearer one is to a saturation level the more difficult it is to increase sales.

It is curious that it is only recently that advertising budgets have been drawn up on the basis of the profitability of the product in question. The basic model for which one is seeking must be of the following form. There must be a relationship between either the amount of advertising, or the share of total advertising on the product group, and the total sales of the product or its share of market.

It is not sufficient to assume that as the total amount of advertising or share of advertising increases there will be a monotonic increase in sales or share of market. In another context Ackoff has shown that in advertising for beer the relationship between total sales and total advertising may be of the form shown in Fig. 47. But whatever the nature of the relationship, a relationship there must be, for life is reasonable and rational. The first step is to try to derive this.

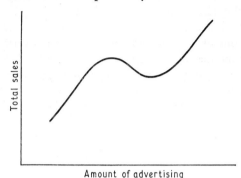

Fig. 47. Relationship between sales and advertising in a beer market

Fig. 48. Relationship between total sales income and its contribution to profits

The second step is to estimate the relationship between the profits stemming from a product and the total sales of the product, without taking account of the cost of achieving the sales view. Unless there are curiosities in the cost function, this relationship will be as shown in Fig. 48.

The third step is to estimate the cost of achieving these sales. This can be derived from Fig. 49 and we would then have a relationship which gives the cost of sales and the profitability stemming from the sales as in Fig. 49.

Clearly these approaches are naïve. They take no account of other forms of sales promotion apart from advertising and they assume that the effectiveness of advertising is measured by its cost. Packaging, display, distribution, product quality, special offers and promotions, activities of salesmen all play their part and a structured model relating these together must

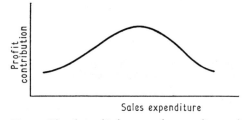

Fig. 49. The relationship between sales expenditure and
contribution to profits

be deduced. Warner has proposed a general model to show the way in which patterns of causes and effects interact as illustrated in Fig. 50.

The model which is depicted in Fig. 50 is an attempt to show the interplay of factors within a total marketing concept and shows the way in which a prototype model can be evolved on the basis of practical knowledge and study. As can be seen the first decision which is taken is that of the amount of advertising which is evaluated in terms of the impact it makes, the attitudes and dispositions of the consumers and the competitive effects of other advertising. These dispositions are affected by premiums and offers, price, distribution, display and the activities of the sales force. In each case all these factors are counterbalanced by competitive effects. The final basic input of the model are the characteristics of the product which have to be critically compared with the consumer's own requirements.

Looking at Fig. 50 one can indicate some of those areas in which significant research has been carried out. At the point of sale, premiums, offers, and retail promotions experiments have been made in the food industry which show the effect of these premiums and offers on sales not only in the short term but also the long-term market gain. It must be confessed that frequently these effects are obscured and one often has the feeling that these expenditures are undertaken by the marketer merely as an insurance, because he is so afraid of what will happen if he ceases to market in this way and yields some sales to a competitor. The effect of a sales force on total sales has been studied in the food industry in Britain and in the American textile industry. For example a study was carried out of the orders booked by salesmen selling fabrics in the garment industry. Customers were classified according to the numbers of successive seasons in which they had bought from the salesman. It was noted that there was a high loss rate; over half the customers who bought for the first time in any one season failed to buy in the following season and of those who did another half failed to buy for the third successive season. On the other hand the size of the orders made by most customers who remained loyal to the company increased markedly from season to season. Although it is not possible yet to tell a sales force how it should occupy its time, it was possible within the terms of this study to show the sales force what were the break-even points in the different strategies they might adopt. For example it could be shown that the long-term effect of increasing the number of new customers in a particular season by, say, ten per cent

K

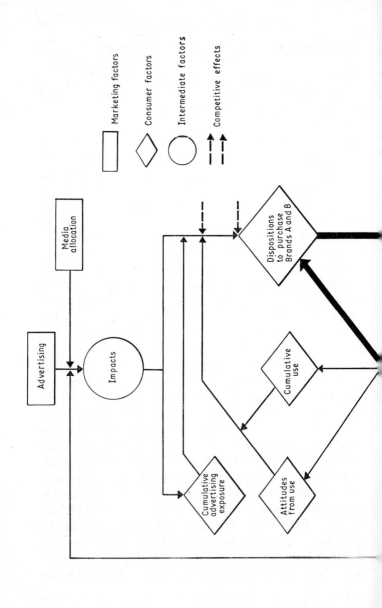

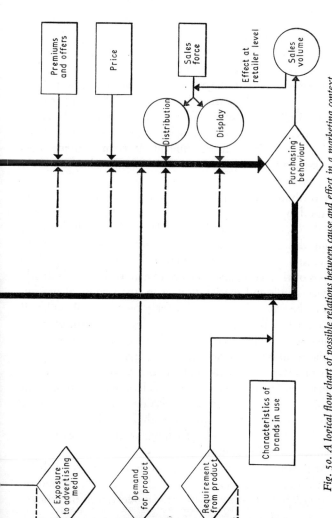

Fig. 50. A logical flow chart of possible relations between cause and effect in a marketing context (From a private report by B. L. Warner of Metra-Sigma Martech.)

would be equal to the long-term effect of retaining first season customers who might otherwise be lost to the second season and increasing this percentage by twenty per cent. The sales force could then decide which was more likely to be achieved as a result of a switch of effort. Equally it was possible to see the relative effectiveness of obtaining more customers or of increasing the sizes of the order from the first season customer, the second season, the third season and so on. In these problem areas the possible results of a particular form of effort cannot be shown and one has to rely on the subjective assessments of the sales force of what is relatively easier or relatively more difficult. It is in deriving these break-even productivities that some significant improvements have been made.

Distribution display has been studied on an experimental method by increasing and decreasing self-service stands in retail stores in certain towns. The interesting result that stems from this is that unless these stands are very frequently checked on by a salesman they will become occupied by goods of rival companies. Hence to gain real effect from self-service stands and special displays in stores constant pressure has to be exerted by the sales force on the retail outlet. In addition it could be seen that the sales, in a town, of goods which were subject to special display were increased not only in the retail outlets in which the displays were operating but also in other outlets throughout the town; this means, of course, that these displays are first of all acting as an advertising medium, and secondly are affecting the loop of actual purchasing behaviour compared with disposition to purchase, that is a constant running feedback of personal experience against external pressures.

At present, in marketing, a great deal of research is being carried out on the separate factors shown in Fig. 50, and the basic task is, first, to see whether the model is realistic structurally, that is does it give logical links between the variables involved, and secondly to impose number and quantity in the model for this is a structure of a model which still lacks quantity.

The question of how numbers can be derived which estimate the importance of the cause–effect relationships outlined in the flow-chart type model (Fig. 50) is still the subject of a deal of discussion. Briefly the two schools of thought are those which might be labelled the microcosmic and the macrocosmic. The microcosmic school believes that it is only possible, by experiment and by analysis, to derive the separate relationships, as indicated above, which when conjoined together make up the model. The macrocosmic school believes that it is not possible or desirable to try to work out these micro-relationships but that one should take the overall situation and derive by statistical analysis and carefully designed experiments the actual quantitative values pertaining to them. The subject is too much in its infancy for any one school to know that it is right. It is unfortunate that solutions to marketing problems can tend to be marketed like the products with which they are concerned. One does not often find in the literature of the subject calm, rational, critical discussions of the advantages and disadvantages of methods which are proposed.

There remains the large problem of the use of gaming theory in decision making. Theory and practice seldom go hand in hand in equal stages of development in any part of O.R. In many areas of decision-making research, the theory is far from developed and one is still groping for first measure. This is certainly true of much work in marketing. In other parts of the subject, theories have been derived which outstrip their application and usefulness. In these situations, there is always the danger of scientists with a particular tool walking around looking for problems which it will fit. Research in the theory of games tends to be of this kind, but it is of such interest that perhaps the reader will bear with a short description.

The theory of games is devoted to considering strategies which competitors should adopt, assuming they each know the outcome of various alternative joint decisions which they may take. For example, suppose we have two opponents A and B who each have two alternative courses of action open to them. There will then be four possible outcomes to the situation depending on whether A has chosen decision 1 or 2 and B has chosen decision 1 or 2. These outcomes could be as illustrated in the following table where the numbers show the amount which B must pay to A given the two decisions which they have taken.

		B	
		1	2
A	1	− 25	10
	2	25	− 5

As can be seen from this table, if A adopts decision 1, he may gain 10 but he may lose 25. On the other hand if A takes decision 2, he may lose 5 but he may gain 25. Looked at from A's point of view, if he takes strategy 1 he may gain more or lose more than on strategy 2.

On the other hand from B's point of view, on strategy 1 he stands to gain or to lose equally heavily, while the results of strategy 2 will be less extreme. What then should these two do? This is a very simple example of the theory of games, from which it can be shown that both A and B should adopt what is called a mixed strategy. This stems from the fact that if A always takes the same decision, for example decision 2 because he stands to gain more, then B would always reply, given that he understands that A is always going to take decision 2, by taking decision 2 and consequently game by game B would gain 5 units per game.

On the other hand if A decides to opt for decision 1 constantly B will opt for decision 2 constantly and will also gain 5 units per game. The only way that A can win anything is to adopt a mixed strategy and vary decision 1 or decision 2. The same argument applies to B's own thinking. The theory of games can evaluate how frequently A should take decision 1 compared with decision 2, and how frequently B should take decision 1 compared with decision 2. If they each play their optimum strategies, it can be shown that they will stabilize at the situation in which in the long run A should play decision 1 six times out of thirteen and B should play decision 1, three times out of thirteen.

The essence of the strategy of both A and B is to select from their two alternative decisions at random, in the given proportions, for if the competitor can foresee one's decision he is bound to win that particular play of the game. If the competitors adopt what is for both of them in their terms an optimum strategy, then out of 169 (being 13 × 13) plays of the game the expected frequencies with which the four different combinations of strategies are taken are—

The value of the game to A is therefore

$$18(-25) + 60\,(10) + 21\,(25) + 70\,(-5) = 325,$$

over 169 plays or an average of $\dfrac{325}{169} = \dfrac{25}{13}$ per play.

The theory of games has developed a very complete theory for dealing with situations of this sort, even for a large number of opponents, and the theory itself is relatively well founded so long as we are in what is called a zero sum game. By a zero sum game is meant one in which the sum total of the gains and losses of all the players, at every play of the game, is zero. As can be seen in the above example, in every game either A pays B or B pays A and so the gain of one is the loss of the other and the total is zero. In practice, however, many competitive situations are of a non-zero sum type. The total gains or losses are not constant or zero at each play of the game. There may be some situations in which, depending on which each takes, the total trans-shipment is not constant. For example in a marketing situation, if the figures involved in the game between two competitors are the total volume of sales stemming from different relative expenditures on advertising, the total market may be affected by total advertising and we would not be in a zero sum situation. Some game theory has been developed to deal with problems of international relations and the work of Rapoport at the University of Michigan is important in this area.

These last two chapters have shown the skeleton of some work being carried out in what are the two most important and fastest growing areas of operational research. In both of these one is trying to evolve structure and quantity. It is often difficult to derive *a priori* models of cause and effect against which analysis will enable one to place numbers. Sometimes it is also difficult to carry out controlled experiments in order to deduce the form of the cause–effect relationship, particularly in the marketing problem, and also when studying decisions taken in allocating effort in research and development, where the research director has (at present implicitly) to balance the interests of the research scientist with the potential pay-off if the research is successful and with the probability that the research will succeed in a given time.

In addition there is the sub-problem of deciding what different and alternative lines of approach to take in a research, where the potential of the end-product depends on the particular alternative. It is an interesting paradox that the two most unstructured and unmeasured problems facing the O.R. scientist at present lie at opposite ends of the management spectrum—research and marketing.[1]

[1] A general discussion of the use of models in marketing is contained in MERCER, A., Applications of O.R. in Marketing, *Op. Res. Q.*, Vol. 16, No. 3.

VIII

SIMULATION

As the reader will have noticed, the emphasis in this discussion of the approach of the operational research worker to the study of the consequences of decisions has been on three steps. The first has been the gaining of a real understanding of what is going on, the second has been the use of this understanding to build a structured quantified set of relationships which express the cause and effect in the decision situation and the third step has been the careful implementation of this model to check whether the assumptions and the structure are justified.

A critical stage is, naturally, the derivation of the consequences of alternative courses of action by the manipulation of the model. Sometimes this is straightforward, for the model is essentially a first statement of measures relevant to alternative actions. At other times, as for example in queueing and in linear programming, the resolution of the model involves a series of mathematical statements. Some of the mathematics can be very sophisticated and at times the handling of the large quantities of data involved in the mathematics may require standard computer programmes to be derived. There are of course, in addition, those investigations in which the structure of the model is derived and verified by means of statistical analyses, since one is dealing with a probabilistic rather than a deterministic situation.

But mathematics does not always prove the only or the best way to solve the equations, and then one has to derive an alternative approach. In other situations, it may not be possible to state the problem in mathematical terms because, although one can state it conceptually, the translation from concepts into the mathematics is too complex to be handled. In both these situations, methods have been derived under the general heading of simulation which are now recognized as being of importance.

At one time scientists resorting to simulation wore a hunted look as they thought that resorting to simulation was a confession of mathematical incompetence. But normally, even in situations where it is not absolutely necessary, because of a breakdown of the mathematics, the simulation approach may well be adopted. The methods of simulation can be used in three main fields: (1) situations in which the mathematical and statistical problems are too complex to be dealt with and alternative methods have to be derived; (2) situations in which the time needed for the research worker to gain an adequate understanding of what is going on would be so long, that the real-life situation has to be imitated and speeded up; (3) situations in which it is not possible to gain practical experience because one is dealing with problems which have not yet arisen.

Because of the importance of simulation processes and because also the way in which the O.R. scientist is working when using a simulation approach is in manner closely akin to that of his colleagues in the practical sciences, we are devoting a chapter of this book to what is a technique approach. The other techniques used in operational research as can be seen, are mathematical and statistical, and these methods have a long history and are well documented elsewhere. There is one first-class general work on simulation approaches to which the reader should go for a full discussion.[1]

[1] TOCHER, K. D., *The Art of Simulation* (E.U.P.).

Beating the Mathematics

The first example comes from the mining industry and is a case study of the use of simulation methods in deciding on the principles to be adopted when installing special emergency procedures for use in collieries.

The problem here was to estimate, given the communication systems available in coal mines, what would be the effect of these systems in clearing a colliery in an emergency. The method used by the team was to visit collieries with different forms of telephone system and to study the use of these systems in day-to-day operation. For, with mining regulations and technology as they are at present, there is no possibility of installing special hooters or sirens for use underground in an emergency. When an emergency arises the message has to be transmitted through the pit by the normal telephone system.

The team spent some time at the telephone switchboard logging all calls made on the system and from this they built up a picture of the delays which might be expected. These are of two sorts. There are the natural delays involved in the time it takes a man working underground to hear a phone, to walk to it and to answer it. There are in addition the delays which arise because some telephones are not answered at all. It was apparent at an early stage of this investigation that one of the problems which would become serious, was that the number of unanswered calls on a pit telephone system is significantly high.

The next stage was to examine for each of the collieries visited the warning routine which the pit would adopt. In some the routine would be to telephone to the coal faces and to give the message to the men there. The management would have to rely on them to come out through the pit and bring all other workers with them. Another routine would be to telephone each district of the pit and speak to the deputy (the foreman) and to rely on him to work around his district and make sure that all his men were evacuated.

Whatever routine would be adopted in the pit, the next step in the investigation was to take a map of the colliery, to mark on it the work places of the underground miners and to try and estimate how long the telephone system would take for the routine to be carried out. The difficult problem, as has been stated, was the existence of unanswered calls. It was because of this that it was necessary to derive a simulation approach. The method evolved by the team can be shown in the following simple example.

Suppose we want to know how long it is likely to take to get an answer to the telephone from a certain coal face. In order to get through to the coal face we can either ring direct with a probability of answer of say fifty per cent, or we can, if we fail to get an answer, ring a neighbouring point for which the probability of answer has been observed to be seventy per cent, and get them to send a runner. If the neighbouring point fails to answer then we may have to ring a third point for which say the probability of answer has been observed to be eighty per cent and get them to send a runner. If there is still no answer we would have to send a runner from the telephone exchange itself.

This can be shown in flow chart form (*see* page 142, percentages represent the chances of the event occurring and numbers the time taken for the event).

We would then work to the following routine. Take a first set of random numbers, with a fifty per cent chance of a particular result (for example, toss a coin). Draw one number out of this set and if the result occurs, we say the point has answered and the time is two minutes. This is the end of that trial. Now start a second trial and draw another random number. We may find the point has not answered. We now wait three minutes after which we give up, and try the second phone. For this point we have a set of random numbers with a seventy per cent chance of answer and thirty per cent chance of no answer. We draw a number from this and find that there is an answer. We have now a total time of five

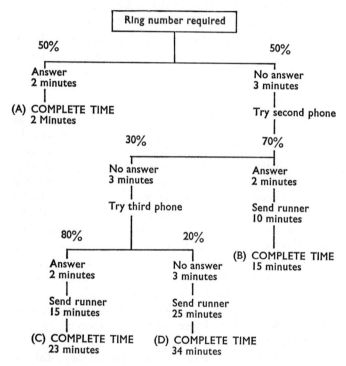

minutes to get to the second phone and another ten minutes for a runner to get across to the coal face making a total, in this trial, of fifteen minutes. In this way we carry out a large number of trials and get a pattern of response. Sometimes we shall get to the coal face very quickly. Other times we may have to give up and send a runner all the way when we shall require a total time of thirty-four minutes to get the message to the coal face.

In the simple example quoted, we could, of course, work out the chances of arriving at each of the four destinations, (A), (B), (C) or (D)—

(A) Probability   = Complete time 2 min.
(B) Probability 0.5×0.7 = Complete time 15 min.
(C) Probability $0.5 \times 0.3 \times 0.8$ = Complete time 23 min.
(D) Probability $0.5 \times 0.3 \times 0.2$ = Complete time 34 min.

$$\text{Overall average time} = \begin{aligned} & 0.5 \times 2 \\ & +0.35 \times 15 \\ & +0.12 \times 23 \\ & +0.03 \times 34 \\ \hline & = 10 \text{ minutes} \end{aligned}$$

But these arithmetical approaches will not be useful in a large pit, with many telephones, where we may want to experiment with different alternatives. Hence we will treat each of the points to which we have to get a message in the same experimental way. From this we build up a cumulative relationship which shows the percentage of the men warned in any given time. For each trial which we carry out the random numbers are allowed to break in the appropriately weighted random fashion and so we get a series of cumulatives as shown in Fig. 51.

In this approach it is possible to estimate what would be the effect on the total warning time of changing the telephone system either by putting in new telephones or re-siting old ones. It was also possible to look at the principles of the layout of underground telephone systems, which in many coal mines use sub-exchanges underground, and to see the extent to which these sub-exchanges were impeding communication.

This, then, is an example of the way in which a model can be built up which does not have a mathematical form. By means of the manpower map and the observation of the performance of the existing telephone systems the team was

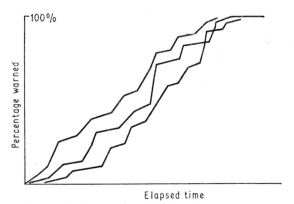

Fig. 51. The relationship between elapsed time and the percentage of men warned in a colliery

able to build up an experimental system from which they could derive estimates of how telephone systems were likely to react in an emergency.

Gaining an Understanding

One of the problems which arise in scheduling steel production is the variability and unpredictability which occur during the process. The work of Tocher at United Steel Company, Sheffield, has pioneered the development of simulation in the production field. The problem is that in the process of steel production, at the successive stages of the process, there is not only great variability in the times needed to complete a given process, but also there is some lack of sureness that the product emerging from each stage will in fact be suitable for the order for which it is nominally being produced. In addition the handling facilities between successive stages of the production process may themselves be complex. In these circumstances the derivation of the optimum capacity at each of the successive stages is far too complex a problem to be solved by straight mathematical equations. In order to gain an understanding of the principles of controlling the flow of steel through such a process it is necessary for the research team to speed up real time and to learn at a faster rate than real time would permit. Hence the group at United Steel has fabricated an imitation steel mill. Those controlling the steel production flow in this imitation mill are presented with the same information in roughly the same form as they would be in real life. The generation of orders, which form the basis of the order book from which all production stems, is based on actual orders received. The times that successive stages of the process will take in any particular case, are generated by samples of random numbers taken from the appropriate statistical distributions; these distributions are based on observation. The movement of in-process work from one process to another is, again, based on actual studies of operations showing the way in which locomotive and crane drivers are likely to work. Faced with this situation, the team can run the hypothetical steel mill according to different principles and thus may rapidly gain an understanding of the basic factors affecting steel flow. Hence, one can show the principles on which steel production should be controlled, with all the possibilities of automation of this control process, and in addition one can show the likely gain to be obtained from providing extra capacity in the different stages of the production process. This is a fearfully complicated and complex problem, and the United Steel Group have been in the forefront in developing simulation methods with a firm theoretical basis.

L

Of a similar, although much more simple, nature, are some studies being carried out at the University of Lancaster into the principles which should govern the admission of patients into a hospital. To a certain extent the problem has similarities to the steel mill scheduling problem. There is a waiting list of patients requiring admission to a hospital, the condition of patients is known but it is difficult, at present, to assign to these conditions an index of priority or of need. The impact of admitting certain types of patient with given conditions into a hospital is measured by the length of time which these patients are likely to occupy the facilities, notably the beds, and in addition the demands they are likely to make on the other services of a hospital such as X-ray, surgical theatre and so on. A simulation programme has been formulated by which a hypothetical hospital with a waiting list of patients of different types can be run in different ways. Naturally the wards and the facilities of the hospital have to be specialized according to the types of patient which are being admitted, and these simulation processes are leading to an understanding of the relative capacities which should be provided in the different parts of the hospital together with very rapid information on the likely effect of batches of patients of different sorts in varying conditions being admitted according to differing admission criteria. In this way it will be possible to show the nature of the facilities which should be provided in a hospital in order, for a given expenditure, to maximize patient care, however this is defined. This example points out an underlying difficulty in approaches of this kind. A computer which is carrying out a simulation is virtually an electronic moron. It has to be provided with a completely detailed breakdown to show what it should do when faced with any particular set of circumstances. This forces the experimenter back to first principles. He has to envisage what decision processes would be employed in all the different situations which may be thrown up, by allowing the random numbers and the samples to be generated in the appropriate way. In the present study, for example, it will be necessary to define the need of a patient. How does one match the relative need of a hernia patient who has been waiting in a queue for one year with a patient with a lung complaint who has been waiting only three months? It is necessary, if we are to provide facilities to meet human need, to have some way of comparing different sorts of human need. It is also necessary, of course, to envisage what is likely to happen if different kinds of facility are provided, because there is an interaction between the queue and the facilities. By this, we mean that in many situations, demand will be seen to expand to meet the increase in the provision of a facility. Hence we have to be able to derive ways of distinguishing between what is wanted and what is needed and to show the way in which the positive feedback, which will result from an increase in the provision of facilities, will lead to an increase in the demand or apparent need for them.

Some studies of a rather theoretical nature have been formulated to gain an understanding of the factors influencing mobility of personnel from one organization to another. For example one could formulate a hypothetical management structure of an organization as in Fig. 52.

Suppose we assign to everybody in the structure three indices representing respectively, the year of birth, the year at which they arrived at their present level in the organization, and finally an "ability" index. Suppose we now allow a flow-through of staff to take place according to different promotion and leaving criteria? We may impose on the structure the provision that people under a certain age who have been more than a minimum number of years on a given level will have a random chance, year by year, of leaving the organization. In addition those who reach a certain age will retire.

For all these movements out of the organization there will be a set of promotions taking place. We may assume on the one hand that people will be promoted according to seniority; on the other hand it could be according to their ability index. Finally it could be according to their length of time on the particular level of the organization in question. This can be matched in with a recruitment policy. We may have a policy of recruiting only into certain levels of the organization people with given minimum indices of ability and of maximum age.

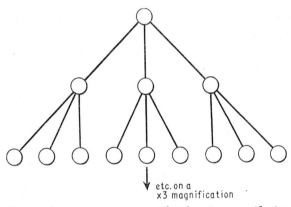

etc. on a
x3 magnification

Fig. 52. A management structure with a three times magnification

For every set of criteria we may employ for promotion there will be an ultimate steady state of this management pyramid, in which there will be an average age and an average index of ability at each level. We may see, for example, that if some people are brought into the organization on a significantly higher level of ability, others will be forced to leave because their chances of promotion are blocked. All these effects can be plotted and the relationships between steady state abilities and ages and the turnover of personnel in the organization can be evaluated.

As can be seen, in this particular section, we have been considering uses of simulation which are, essentially, to gain an understanding of what is really going on. Once we have this understanding it may be possible, then, to formulate the problems in a non-simulated, perhaps in a purely mathematical, form. However in general, the current of opinion at present is that the simulation methods themselves are of more power than the mathematical methods. This is because of their experimental nature and the rapid way in which, given a simulation programme, it is very easy to change the basic conditions and to see what effect this has. In mathematical terms, changing the basic conditions takes one back to the beginning of the mathematics again and the whole theory has to be worked out afresh. This is not so within the terms of a simulation approach. It is in the deriving of general simulation programmes in particular and in the development of computer languages, that the United Steel Company group has done so much pioneering work and has influenced greatly the pattern of development of operational research in this field.

Dealing with the Future

One of the difficulties facing military operational research workers is that, fortunately, the opportunities for collecting live data are few. The principles on which men and weapon systems should be deployed in battle are difficult to derive and field trials and military exercises have only limited usefulness. In addition, there is the problem of deciding the relative merits of proposed new weapons for use in military operations. Since the effect of these weapons depends on their interactions with all other types of weapon, it is not possible to gain an estimate of their overall effectiveness in a battle without actually fighting the battle itself. It is to meet these problems that the British Defence Operational Analysis Establishment, as have most military operational research establishments, derived war games.

War games have a history extending over some thousands of years. In the middle of the seventeenth century Christopher Weikhmann introduced a modification of chess which he called the King's game. In this each player was given thirty pieces that together had fourteen different kinds of move. Over a hundred years later at Prague, Hoechenberger invented a similar game, and a more elaborate modification of chess was devised and introduced in the court of Brunswick in 1780. The object of this game was to attract the attention of young men destined for military service and to lessen the difficulties of instruction; pieces representing battalions of infantry and squadrons of cavalry were moved on a board divided into about 1,600 small squares. These squares were coloured so as to represent different kinds of ground, villages and lakes, etc. This was the first specific use of a game of this nature as a training device and it inspired a number of variations in the latter years of the eighteenth century. This led to the first introduction of *Kriegspiel*, a term which has been used for many years to denote this type of war game. In *Kriegspiel* maps are introduced in place of the ordinary game boards and the maps are themselves divided into squares across which troops are able to move in terms of the configuration of the ground. It was felt, however, by many people, particularly the military, that this particular war game had developed in too complex a fashion and it ended in a blind alley.

Other advances in this kind of war chess were made in Prussia during the early nineteenth century and led to the development of what has come to be regarded as the modern war game. In these games the exercises were conducted on maps and so a wide variety of military situations could be shown. It was agreed by the Prussian Chief of General Staff that every regiment should be supplied with one of these games which were to be used for the tactical training of officers. These games introduced the important variant which distinguishes modern war gaming, namely, that there are two separate maps, one for each army commander showing only the opposing troops which he can actually see. Consequently there was a need for the introduction of an umpire and it is this distinguishing feature which makes the real break with war chess. For in war chess each commander, as in normal chess, has full information about the deployment of his opponents' pieces. In the development of the war game it was recognized that most of the problems of the army commander, as the Duke of Wellington observed, are those which stem from the fact that he has incomplete information about his opponent's dispositions.

The difficulty which had to be faced by all those who were interested in the development of *Kriegspiel* was that it was impossible to reconcile playability of a game with realism. As has been seen elsewhere in this book, this is a basic difficulty which faces the operational research worker in every decision-making problem. The more realistic we make the models with which we deal, the less likely it is that we shall be able to solve the problems which they represent. In the development of *Kriegspiel* war gaming was modified into the two fields of rigid *Kriegspiel* and free *Kriegspiel*, corresponding to realistic games and playable games. In the realistic games, dice were introduced to represent the effects of chance, and tables, charts and calculations were produced to show how the movement of troops would actually take place across the board. In the free *Kriegspiel* in general, the result of any engagement is shown not by allowing probabilities to break through the throw of a die, but by the subjective assessment of an umpire which enabled games to be played at a much faster speed than in the rigid *Kriegspiel*.

During the years between the First and the Second World Wars, the German army developed war gaming quite extensively. The spring offensive of 1918 was rehearsed through war gaming and in World War Two the invasions of France in 1940 and of the Ukraine in 1941, and also plans for an invasion of England were developed as a result of extensive war gaming. C. J. Thomas has given an account of the history of war games.[1]

At the present time most military establishments have developed such gaming methods to allow themselves the opportunity to win wars without actually fighting, and the Defence Operational Analysis Establishment at Byfleet, Surrey, have derived a war game which is played on a map of Europe. The game is played by two opposing commanders, each of whom have their own terrain maps, extending over about six hundred square feet, and there is a third map which is under the control of the experimenters. The commanders are given forces of different natures, and a defensive battle is fought in which an aggressor is attacking the area held by the defender. The forces consist of support aircraft, artillery, tanks and infantry. The commanders move their troops across the battlefield as in chess. When two elements of opposing forces come in contact with each other, the outcome of the engagement is estimated from trial data which are in the possession of the Operational Research Group. For example, a commander may decide to send an aircraft on observation over a particular part of the enemy territory. From trials data, the umpires will assess the probability that the cloud cover is sufficient for successful photographs to be taken, the probability that the photographs will actually be taken in the right place

---

[1] THOMAS, C. J., The Genesis and Practice of Operational Gaming, *Proc. First Int. Conf. on O.R.* (E.U.P. 1957).

and finally the probability that, given the weapons of the ground forces, the aircraft will be shot down. Consequently when an aircraft is sent on patrol by one commander, the umpires work out all these probabilities, based on their trials data. They then sample at random from appropriate weighted probabilities and inform the commander what has happened to the aircraft in this particular instance. If the aircraft has been shot down, they inform the ground forces on the other side that an aircraft did come on patrol and has been shot down.

Again, where tank forces come into battle with each other, given the number and size of the opposing forces, the use of trials data, which will give the results of the contest in probability form, can allow the umpires to make a similar random sample and tell the opposing commanders how many tanks have been destroyed on their own side, how many they can assume have been destroyed on the opponents' side. The commanders can then make their further dispositions.

The commanders who take part in the game are serving officers from the army and it is interesting that during the game they show some of the same stress symptoms that they would in real battle. To this extent they, like the steel managers in the steel simulation example, are reacting as the constructors of the game would wish, for the game is clearly lifelike to them. The other advantage of the war game is that it gives the designers the opportunity not only to assess the alternative virtues of different methods of controlling fighting troops in the field, but also to assess the possible effect of new weapons systems which have not yet been developed. The effect, for example, on a battle of the development of a new anti-tank gun having a certain range accuracy and armour penetration can be derived by seeing how battles would be fought and would result if certain numbers of these guns were available to one side. It is rather like trying to see the effect on a game of chess of introducing a piece with a different characteristic of movement. This can only be derived by playing a number of games of chess and seeing the effect the new piece has on the performance of one player. Consequently these games serve a twofold purpose. They give the experimenter the opportunity of deriving principles of combat and, more important, they serve as a guide to research and development of new weapons.

There is however one difficulty under which these games labour at present. This is the extreme time which the war game takes. The present time scale is roughly three times the equivalent real life time. It is still worth while spending the time on the war game, even under these circumstances, because, of course, there is no comparable opportunity to obtain battle data. Indeed even were there battles going on continuously from which information could be derived, the game would still give the opportunity for controlled experimentation and for envisaging future operations.

As can be seen this military game is almost entirely non-mathematical in character. It is very much like a laboratory experiment. The map over which the commanders fight is very much the terrain map which they would be faced with in a battle situation. The information would come to them as in a battle. The results of engagements are based on trials of weapons under controlled conditions. Consequently by matching practical experience derived on special conditions with situations which have not yet arisen, the war games provide an opportunity for the military operational research worker to act in very much the same way as his colleagues in a physics or chemistry laboratory.

In those situations where both sides in a conflict are carrying out gaming processes, provided they have the same basic information about their own and their opponents' forces, there is a possibility that they will come to the same conclusion regarding the result of a particular action. This may lead to a reduction in the probability of wars breaking out in a major fashion since wars, in general, are only carried out when both sides think they have a significant chance of actually winning. The Cuban episode of 1962 is a possible point in question. It will be recalled that the Americans discovered that on Cuba there had been a build-up of missile bases by the Russians. A Russian fleet was sailing west to reinforce this base, and the Americans were undecided what action should be taken with regard to this fleet. It seemed that a major war was in the offing. Suddenly the Russian fleet pulled away and retired eastwards and that was that. It would be interesting to know what really happened in the Pentagon and in the Kremlin. One might, however, conjecture that the military scientists on both sides had gamed the situation and had come to the same conclusion, namely that the optimum course of action for both sides was for the Russians to withdraw.

The methods of simulation then, can be seen to have very great power for the operational research worker. The mathematical and statistical approaches to model building yield experimental systems in which optimum solutions are sought by mathematical means. The great advantage of simulation methods is that they give the O.R. worker a feeling for the real nature of the problem which he is dealing with. The influence of the United Steel simulation approach is pervasive, and it is probably in the extension of simulation procedures to operational research methods that we shall see the much more significant development of the science than simply in the mathematical and statistical processes as they now stand.

IX

HOW TO FAIL AND
HOW TO SUCCEED

THE operational research scientist works under both the handicap and the advantage of not being able to provide for himself the facilities which are necessary for his research. In this he is different from his colleagues in other sciences who have laboratories provided within which they are free, in broad terms, to carry out what research they wish. The operational research scientist always has to persuade the owner of the laboratory to let him in to carry out his studies, and in order to do this the O.R. scientist has to sell his wares. This creates the danger that we may present operational research as a glittering catalogue of successes which is entirely unacquainted with failure. Every operational research scientist knows that, as a research activity, O.R. itself is, like all research, cradled in failure. Unless an operational research group is acquainted with failure in the projects it studies, then the projects have been badly selected and are not of a research nature. This is not to say we shall be happy when we have one hundred per cent failure, but rather that we should be suspicious when we have one hundred per cent success.

Hence although the operational research worker as a research scientist walks hand in hand with failure, he must be aware of those circumstances which will lead to the failure, otherwise avoidable, of an investigation. It is the purpose of this chapter to suggest circumstances in which failure will be ensured and also to indicate those conditions which seem helpful to promote success.

Let us consider first of all the conditions which seem to lead to failure. The first of these concerns the way in which the team regards the problem which it is studying. In general the problems which management face are ill defined, particularly from an operational research point of view. For the reason we are given problems is, often, that management itself realizes that it is faced with symptoms and wants to know underlying causes. Consequently, in these terms, the first definition of the problem will not read like an examination question. We have to find what the problem is and we have then to make a variety of choices about the way in which we shall approach it. We must remember that there is a large subjective element in the way in which all teams look at problems. Each of us has our own subconscious way of regarding problems, and we must not think that they exist somewhere in the company in an absolute form, as revealed truth. When we have an appreciation of what we think the problem really is, there seem to be two ways in which we tackle it. It is, first of all, extremely unlikely that we shall find an exact solution to the exact problem. There will be a level of approximation. We can either find an exact solution to the approximate problem or an approximate solution to the exact problem. In circumstances of great desperation we may even have to content ourselves with approximate solutions to approximate problems. The operational research worker who is bedazzled by mathematical technique (he is more often the man who does not understand the technique properly, rather than one who understands it well) will attempt to formulate an approximation to the real problem to which he will derive an exact solution. He may then find, when he presents his answer to management, that the reaction of the executive is: "Thank you very much, this is very interesting but it is not my problem." This reply often hurts the operational research worker's finer feelings, because he has derived, sometimes under conditions of great mathematical difficulty, an exact solution to a problem, of which he is rather proud. But it stands no chance at all of implementation if what he presents is a solution to a problem which does not exist so far as the executive is concerned. It is probably rather better in general terms (we realize it is difficult to generalize) to try and derive an approximate solution to the exact problem. In fact, in these situations, the operational research worker will often have to spend some time on the formulation of the problem and on *understanding* the real structure of what is going on. This is a point we shall return to later.

It is difficult to over-emphasize the importance of understanding the real problem and of ensuring that the manager concerned recognizes this as his problem. This means that there must be continuing contact with management during this gestation period, which will end with the birth of a problem, rather than with the birth of an answer to it.

A second reason for failure lies in the competence of the team. There is a fashionable feeling in operational research that techniques are unimportant. We are certainly right to concentrate our thinking on the formulation of problems and of understanding the real structure of what is going on in management situations. The author often finds that his own graduate students will avidly devour the mathematical and statistical techniques which are presented to them, but will switch off their minds when they go on to consider the way in which these techniques are employed in practice. These two attitudes reflect the two sins into which an operational research worker can fall in the matter of his techniques. It must be confessed that too many operational research workers fail because they are incompetent in the mathematical and statistical techniques of their subject. One suspects that many of those who decry the use of techniques in real-life problems do so simply because they are aware that they do not understand the techniques. Often when we have described, understood and defined a real-life problem properly, we become aware that there is a particular body of experience expressing itself in mathematical terms which can be used in this kind of problem. O.R. workers are sometimes unaware of specialist knowledge which is available in other disciplines, such as economics or engineering or sociology, which would be of use in the particular problem they are tackling. Most O.R. workers can remember occasions when an operational research scientist, after spending a year or more studying a particular problem, has produced a solution which expresses something, for example an indifference curve, about which the economists knew a quarter of a century ago. There is a danger that through using mixed teams in O.R. we come to assume that the mixed team expresses the whole of the available knowledge we have about the universe in which we operate. There is also the twin danger that, when considering the competence of operational research teams, we shall include people who are over-competent in a particular speciality. There are groups who think of operational research in terms of a specific technique. One or two extremists even say that what we think of as traditional O.R. is dying and in a few years time it will become recognized that the whole subject comes down to linear programming and computers. It is difficult to understand this attitude and it is this approach of over-competence in a particular speciality which might bastardize the science into something which it is not. This threat is present in some of the failures with which the subject has been associated.

A third feature of situations which fail, is one which intimately affects the implementation of the actual solution. For we may find at the end of a study that we have been investigating a situation which is relatively robust. One has the feeling that over a wide range of decisions taken in most organizations there is an associated range of choice through which it does not really matter what is done. If this were not so the bankruptcy rate would be much higher than it is. It is this kind of decision-making situation which the operational research worker must avoid. For example, in inventory control, one may lavish calculus on trying to find the minimum point of a horizontal straight line. We have to be careful that we are studying problems which are sensitive, but we also have to remember, of course, that sensitivity should be expressed in absolute and not in relative terms. In some linear programming situations, for example, the difference between the worst possible solution and the best possible solution may only be less than five per cent. In small-scale problems the five per cent may not be worth worrying about, but in large-scale problems it is. In the terms of the oil industry, for example, two per cent of infinity is still infinity and is worth striving for. A question we have to ask at the beginning of an O.R. investigation, to avoid this sort of failure is simply "does it really matter?"

Implementation lies at the heart of the matter, for unless we get a solution implemented we have failed. To avoid failure, we have to think in terms of implementation, and this is not something to be considered when the problem is solved but rather at the very beginning of the investigation itself.

In considering the question of implementation we have to ask how the organization works. The author has seen a number of problems to which quite impressive solutions have been proposed, which cannot be implemented, because the company does not work that way. In this situation what has happened is that the O.R. team have raced too quickly through their understanding of the problem. The importance of understanding the situation in which we operate cannot be over-emphasized and it is only when we understand the situation and the way management works in the particular organization involved that we can really think in terms of the sorts of solution that are going to be usable.

Some years ago the author was concerned with a study in the American textile industry. In the particular company in question there were a number of textile mills which were spinning yarn and weaving cloth against a running order book. The raw cotton was bought on behalf of all the mills by a wholly owned subsidiary which, in the light of the current order position in the different mills, bought raw cotton of the appropriate grade and staple which was then shipped to the mills to be blended prior to spinning the yarn. There is a variety of blends from which the same type of yarn can be spun and hence there was a degree of flexibility in the activities of the buying corporation. The mill managers were judged by the profitability of their mills and approximately thirty per cent of their total costs was raw material and over these costs they had no control. It was the mill managers who jointly financed the research.

The buying corporation employed two men who worked their way across the cotton fields of the United States, starting in May in the south-east and finishing in December in the west. These men bought in a casual fashion, virtually by jotting down numbers on the back of an envelope. Each evening they would telephone their headquarters and give the information about their purchases and would get an up-to-date run-down on the present order position. The crucial feature of their operation was the special way in which they classified the cotton fibre into grade and staple. It was apparent from the beginning of the study that it was far more important for the company to retain the services of these two men, because of their great skills in classification, than it was to devise a highly accurate system for testing how much cotton of

M

each sort should be bought at what price. Ideally one would have liked to have provided a solution with all this information in it. Looking at the practical situation however, one had to work, from the beginning, towards a solution which was capable of being given over the telephone to two people who would never fill more than the back of an envelope. Hence the implementation of the results started with the recognition of the form that the solution had to take.

It is essential to understand the way in which the management team of an organization thinks and acts. One thing that is common to all management teams is that they do not want to be surprised. One observes an operational research worker striding into the office of the managing director, waving a piece of paper, and exclaiming "Are you going to be surprised by this!" There is no worse introduction to an O.R. solution. The one thing the managing director does not want to have happen to him is to be told that he will be surprised that something has been going on in his organization. He will feel his competence and his authority affronted. We may, of course, get surprising results, but everyone must be aware of what the results are going to be. The problem here is that the executives to whom we report should be aware of the problem we are solving and should be aware of the sorts of answer that might come out, however unlikely they may be.

A final reason for the difficulty of implementation may well be that the O.R. team is located in the wrong part of the organization. There is no overall answer to where operational research should be and I shall return to this problem in a later part of this chapter. We must remember that in reporting the results of an O.R. study we are injecting into the body politic of the organization something which, for action to take place, must get through to the channels of power in the company. If it is injected into the wrong part it can be

lost and the answer may never get through to the real control
centres of an organization.

Success in operational research stems from three main
fundamentals. The first is the way in which we select a
project, the second is the questions we ask at the beginning of
the project and the third is the extent of the involvement of
management during the research. All else is subsidiary to these
three factors.

Operational research workers have now passed the stage
when they are overwhelmed with gratitude and enthusiasm
simply by being asked to study any problem at all. Operational research teams are now in a position to select projects
from those which are given them and may well suggest
projects themselves. How is this done?

There are two ways in which a team can go about this.
First we can reflect that in operational research we are concerned with the consequences of decisions. Hence we look
around the organizations for decisions in which there is a
real range of choice. The choice may be only limited but it
must exist. Secondly we have to look for those decision-
making situations in which this real choice exists and is
significant. We have mentioned the dangers of trying to find
the minimum points of horizontal straight lines and so we
have to ask: does it really matter? Is this a decision-sensitive
situation? If it is not, then we must have none of it.

We have to remember that the operational research worker
does not have experience to offer on running the organization
within which the problem is found. All he has is a skill in
observation and in the collection, sorting and analysis of
data. This means that we have to inquire whether real data
exist. If we are dealing with a situation which is only manifest
by opinions then it is probably not one which is worth the
O.R. workers' time in studying. This means that for the
time being we may not be able to study a large number of

situations (in the organization of research or in marketing, in both of which we have decision-sensitive situations) in which the data which express alternative consequences are not presently available.

When we have reached the stage where we are aware that in a decision there is a range of choice, that the choice really matters and there are quantitative data available, we have still to look ahead at implementation. Around every organization there are sacred cow zones with which one meddles at one's peril. We have to ask whether management is willing to contemplate change in this particular part of its activity. Given an affirmative to these four questions there is no reason why we should not go ahead with confidence into an O.R. study.

An example of this is a study which was carried out some years ago for a Company in the manufacturing business. They purchased a raw material on a market in which the availability and price varied significantly over time, and from this raw material a finished good was manufactured and marketed in a highly competitive field. The purpose of the study was to see what decision laws could be erected for dealing with the problem of the purchase of the raw material which was bought on a contract basis and contracts for forward delivery of the material were negotiated at given prices. The problem as posed to the research team was: given a forecast of forward price how far ahead should we be covered with contracts to buy so that in the long run purchasing may be carried out at minimum price? These price forecasts were available in probability form in terms of an upper and lower limit between which the price was expected to lie during any given period for the next eighteen months. Naturally the further ahead one was looking the wider would be the bounds placed on the expected price.

It was found possible to derive a mathematical model of

this operation and from this the answer stemmed in the form of a forward commitment or coverage which should be held at any given time in terms of the price of the raw material at that day. The formula result would be compared with the existing coverage week by week and, when the existing coverage was less than that given by the mathematical model further purchases were made in order to bring the coverage up to the theoretical value. However in terms of the algebra buying and selling are the same and hence it was logical that when the company was over-committed forward, according to the formula, they should be prepared to sell the excess to bring their commitment to the theoretical value. However this they firmly declined to do; their view was they were not in the brokerage business but were solely in business to buy raw material and to manufacture a finished product. So far as they were concerned although it could be shown that the straightforward selling of contracts would give a significant increase in profitability this was something that they were not prepared to do. One has to respect a company's views on those fields in which they are not prepared to operate. Sometimes these are quite capricious and there may seem no reason other than pure emotion for the refusal to move into a certain field. Nevertheless the operational research worker has to recognize these possibilities and the likely reactions of the company before he undertakes a study so that he is not wasting his time.

But sometimes it may be objected that we cannot possibly survey all decision-making situations with these four criteria in mind. What short-cut methods are there? A useful method is to go through an organization with an emotional thermometer and observe where the mercury rises. Where are the battles going on in the organization? Who is fighting whom? What clashes are there that stem from the genuine clash of objectives? We must not regard conflict as something which is bad, *per se*, for much good can come out of the conflict within an organization. We must remember that conflicts do exist and the way in which we organize modern business is such as to build in conflict into situations. Why should this be so?

We divide organizations into departments and impose on them criteria of performance. Production may be judged by the long-run cost expressed in terms of per unit produced. Marketing is judged, curiously, on volume sold rather than on contribution to profits of what is sold. Hence marketing ideally will require a wide range of products available in profusion at every point of sale, while production ideally would like to produce only one single product. To the accountant, inventory is a dirty word and is something which has to be cut. The production manager may want to manufacture for inventory, particularly in times of recession, in order to retain skilled workers. It is just at this time that finance will want to cut inventory in order to keep up the return on the assets of the company. Purchasing is judged by the long-run usage price of the raw materials which are bought in the market irrespective of the effect these raw materials have on the costs and throughput of the production process.

When companies operate separate factories, which produce overlapping ranges of product, these factories, if they are judged on their profitability or on the return on the assets involved in them, will be competing with each other and hence there is another source of conflict. The large modern company is not a happy band of brothers marching into battle under a banner carried by the Chairman of the Board, but is rather a snarling guerrilla band, whose members sometimes lavish on each other tactics which they would never dream of using on the company's rivals, because they would be counted unethical.

These conflicts are caused by imposing, on the different

parts of an organization, criteria of performance which contradict. In resolving these conflicts and deriving measures of performance between which different parts of the organization can operate and increase the profitability of the company as a whole, the operational research worker has a rich field for activity. This is a particularly rewarding way of discovering areas of a company's operations in which O.R. is likely to be of assistance. Of course, in carrying out studies on the battlefield of a company one is liable to get wounded by friendly bullets. The operational research worker who seeks to carry out investigations in this field has to develop a defensive armour, or at least a philosophy which enables him to shrug off the slings and arrows of outrageous friends.

Having evolved an area for study which is likely to be useful and solvable, the O.R. worker must then ask certain questions about the way in which he should carry out the study. There are three of these. The first is, simply, the question of when the answer is wanted. There is a temptation to the executive to reply that he wants the answer tomorrow, but a company which always wants all answers by tomorrow is one that is likely to be run so inefficiently as not to be worthy of study. The question does exist, however, of when answers should be produced. Some O.R. projects fail because the answers are produced so late, that the organization has changed or the people who wanted this study carried out have gone into other fields. We have to remember that there is no linear relationship between the amount of truth we discover and the time we spend on an investigation. We may well discover eighty per cent of the answer in twenty per cent of the total time, and in these circumstances we have to ask ourselves whether it is worth going on. As practical problem solvers we seek to improve the profitability of the organizations which use us, rather than to act as dispassionate passionless creatures in white coats who are trying to find the last syllable of recorded truth. Timing of course is related to the second question, which is that of the degree of accuracy of the results which is needed. Looking at the organization to which we are reporting and bearing in mind the accuracy of the basic data lead us to try to formulate an estimate of this. Often figures which look remarkably correct when appearing in the black and white of a printed volume, gradually lose their appearance of correctness and dissolve into a mist of ambiguity when one gets back to the source of the data themselves. The treatment of costs and revenue by the accountant also falls into this category. We have to be very careful to inquire into the way in which accountants have treated figures for allocating overheads, the allocation of revenues, the approach to depreciation and obsolescence and so forth, before we can feel we are attributing as much accuracy to the data as they themselves warrant.

The final question which requires to be asked is that of the applicability of the solution. We have to ask: "in this sort of organization what form must the solution take to be usable?" Every company has different ways in which it is used to work and we have to produce answers which are capable of being employed within the general decision-making system and the decision-making philosophy of the particular company concerned. It is not a question of adapting our solution when we have discovered it so that it takes the form of something which can be used in the organization. The O.R. worker always has to remember that he is not dealing with problems of examination question type. In examination questions all the information which is produced is true, there is no redundancy, there is no deliberate attempt at ambiguity and there is a clear statement of what sort of answer is required. In real life we are not dealing with situations in which all the information with which we are presented is true; there will be deliberate attempts to falsify and to erect a smoke screen of ambiguity, and the question which is being asked may be obscure. In mathematics one is dealing with problems for which there is a unique solution which will be eternally valid. In operational research we are dealing with problems for which there are many solutions, all of which will have a transient validity. We can, and must, therefore, at the beginning of an O.R. study consider what form the solution should take.

The question which we have to ask in considering the possibilities of successful completion of an O.R. project lies in the whole problem of the relationship of the operational research team and the management of the company in which it is operating. Let us consider first of all the location of operational research in a company. There is no optimum solution, for companies consist of human beings and this is essentially a human problem. However there are some general conditions upon which it is worth reflecting.

Most operational research workers would maintain that the best place for O.R. is to put it in as exalted a position as possible in the management pyramid. Everyone likes to report to the chairman of the board but we have to consider all the essential requirements for the location of a group. It must be, first of all, either within or contiguous to the main stream of the decision-making of the company. It must be intimately associated with the sweat and the battle of management. Secondly it must have access to information. This means it must be in a part of an organization which can get at quantitative data flow. Thirdly it must have access to the corridors of power since it will have to persuade people that its solutions make sense and that decisions should be taken based on these solutions. Fourthly, the O.R. team should be placed in a situation where it can be seen to be having responsibility for the success or failure of the decisions which stem from its conclusions. Finally the O.R. team must have security of tenure. This is absolutely essential if it is not to be nervously casting glances over its shoulder to see when the dagger is going to fall.

To locate an O.R. team in the chairman's or deputy chairman's office will satisfy most of these requirements. However a deputy chairman is a transient figure and the O.R. team may find that they are faced with a rapid change of climate when a sympathetic deputy chairman is replaced by an unsympathetic one. Consequently one has to think carefully before locating O.R. at such a high level in an organization, and equally to consider the competence and maturity of the members of the team. It is all very well to seek to get into the first division of management but this is not going to render the O.R. man much help if he possesses only third division maturity. Reporting to top management means that one is in the big league and one has to be able to think and talk in big league terms.

An alternative to this is to place the operational research team in one of the major departments of the organization such as production and marketing, purchasing, personnel and so on. This gives security of tenure. It gives good access to information within one's own department, but is no guarantee of access to information outside it. The most serious criticism however of this placing is that one can very soon be regarded as the advocate of the particular department in which the O.R. team is located. Although the O.R. worker, as a scientist, may claim that he is completely unbiased and completely objective, sometimes he will unwittingly assume the colour of his surroundings and the biased man who thinks he is unbiased is a far greater danger in an organization than the man who is honestly biased.

In some organizations there is a management services group and it is attractive to think of putting operational research into this. One has to be careful however to inquire

what sort of management services group this is. For in some
organizations it is a chapel of refuge for failed managers. If
this is so, to locate an operational research team within it
would be to implant the kiss of failure on its brow from the
very beginning. However, if management services is a
dynamic thrusting group which is well regarded within the
organization, then it is a very good place for operational
research.

One invitation to failure is to put operational research
within another management speciality. One has seen attempts
to run O.R. within an organization and methods department,
within a method study department and so on. In general
this is not a good way. It is equally bad to put method study
within an operational research group. For these are different
specialities with parity of esteem and to put one within
another is not helpful either to the subordinate or to the
superior.

It will be noted that two possible locations have not been
discussed so far. One is to put operational research within the
research division. At first sight this seems admirable, for the
O.R. worker will be surrounded by fellow scientists and
should thrive in the scientific atmosphere. But some research
departments are more conscious of the calendar than the clock
and are not operating within the main stream of pressure of
the organization. Perhaps this is a reason why O.R. has
succeeded in disappointingly few cases in a research department. The shining example is the outstandingly successful
group at the British Iron and Steel Research Association.

One final possible location for operational research is
within the finance department of the company. Where one
has seen this done it seems to be most successful, provided
that the accounting department is one that does not consist
of elderly gentlemen of both sexes doing ritual dances by
rote, but rather one that looks on accountancy as a discipline

which is capable of significant improvement, is aware of probability and is aware of the contribution that other sciences can make. In this environment the O.R. team may find that they have good access to information throughout the organization, for this is part of the task of a finance department, they will have security of tenure, they will be placed with people who are used to assuming responsibility for the overall health of the organization and finally, because in most organizations finance control is the one thing that is not decentralized, they will find that they will have access direct to the corridors of power. There is much to commend locating operational research within a financial department.

But when all is said and done, at every stage of an operational research study we depend on getting the management involved. It is useful at the beginning of an O.R. study to set up a small management team consisting of one or two directors of the company plus one or two senior managers, to meet month by month with the leader of the O.R. team to discuss the progress of the project. Sometimes not much progress will have been made but it is still worth while holding the meeting. The O.R. manager can present the results so far arising and get the reactions of the senior group. He can present the quantitative data that are emerging and often will be shown by the senior group where the shortcomings lie in the data and what sorts of opinion among those he is getting should be discounted. The O.R. manager carrying out an investigation is quite a nuisance to those who are supplying him with data and who have other jobs to do. If the directors and senior managers are on this O.R. panel the people concerned at lower levels of management will realize that the information they are presenting will go right to the top of the firm and so the time they spend in collecting the information for the O.R. team will not be personally wasted.

Because O.R. is such an interesting activity (it is really difficult for the author to understand why anybody should ever want to do anything else), the senior managers will find themselves getting involved in the O.R. study. They will cease just commenting on results as they come through but will be proposing new lines of attack. They will suggest new areas into which an investigation should proceed and they will be the best of informed advocates for the study. Being associated with the study also will give them some insight into the problems of model building and why the operational research worker goes about his work the way he does. An O.R. study is not one in which there is at its conclusion a sudden unveiling of the statue of truth, but, rather, is a study during which one is gradually chipping away at the confused complex mass of stone with which one is presented until gradually the bones of the solution emerge. A senior management team can often take action in advance of the final report's being written, action which by saving time may also save money or increase profits. But most important of all, when the time comes for a solution to be sold to the rest of the top management, the men who have formed part of the O.R. panel are the best advocates for its selling. If there is any vicious infighting to be done, these senior managers are postgraduates at this task and will be very good allies of the much more timid O.R. manager. There may well be parts of the method which the other directors of the board cannot understand but their reaction will often be: "Well I don't understand what these Greek letters are all about, but George seems to think it's all right and so I'll go along with George."

It is in this sort of approach, of involving management at every stage, that we shall find implementation is something which begins right at the beginning of a study.

During the war the military operational research groups had the great advantage of creating an intimate relationship with command staffs. In particular the chief O.R. scientists were able to give an informed running commentary on the papers which crossed the commanding officer's desk. It is essentially this which O.R. needs now to strive to do in industry and in government. The tendency to create an O.R. establishment which forms a nice part of a management tree may inhibit this close relationship between the O.R. worker and management. What the O.R. scientist has to offer is something which to most managers is strange. It is much easier to refuse to accept an idea which is on paper; when it is proposed personally by its proponent it is much more difficult to reject a new idea out of hand. The O.R. worker himself has as much to gain as the manager by such an intimate association, if not more. He has to learn what the manager's problems are really like. This he can only do by getting under the skin of the problem and seeing what are the real limiting conditions under which the managers operate. Some of these conditions may be peculiar to the management involved and it is only when there is a close personal relationship with mutual trust and even affection on both sides that O.R., in its fullest, most fruitful and rewarding sense, can be carried out.

X

THE PROBLEM OF EDUCATION
AND TRAINING

As can be seen the development of operational research has been through an initial creation of the science in the military field, followed by a rapid development in industry. It is only recently in Britain that the subject has been taken seriously by universities, and we still await any real awakening in government departments.

One of the difficulties which are imposed on universities stems from their internal organization. In the older universities particularly the rigid division of research and teaching into faculties and departments has meant that any department which is striving to expand will always do so at the expense of another. Hence there has been a tendency to erect walls around the departments and faculties. This has meant that the development of interdisciplinary subjects has been inhibited. In general they have been developed by being disguised in such a way that they can be forced within one department. This inevitably leads to the jibe that the universities look on knowledge and the experience and problems in the outside world as being conveniently divided into university departments.

Some universities have managed to escape from this strait-jacket. Birmingham, which pioneered operational research, was the first to do so, and has been followed by London, Hull and more recently the new universities at Lancaster, Strathclyde and Sussex.

A basic problem in creating competent teaching and academic research in operational research is imposed by the shortcomings of present first-degree courses in Britain. We require as entrants to operational research, good scientists from a broad field of engineering, physics, chemistry, economics and social sciences, and the language science of mathematics. It is curious that it is still perfectly possible in the late 1960s, and indeed is thought quite proper, for students to graduate in science without any knowledge or feeling for probability and statistics. Even at school the young student is taught that variability implies a lack of accuracy, and imprecision. A schoolboy, who is experimenting with rolling a ball down an inclined plane in order to evaluate the gravitational constant, will learn to fudge his results. The time he records that the ball takes to roll down the plane is one which will give him the right value of g. So much of science is still taught from a rigid old-fashioned deterministic viewpoint, that the student who is introduced to the study of statistical methods finds he is faced with radically new concepts of thought.

Some universities do teach statistical methods to undergraduates. Others, in their mathematics syllabus, will cover some of the techniques which are useful in operational research. The mathematical and statistical techniques which need to be learnt as a basis for competence in operational research all fall conceptually within the level of an undergraduate course.

The main burden of teaching the embryo operational research worker has to be carried out either within the large industrial groups which can afford to spend time and effort on this task, or alternatively, in the universities where, when suitably combined with research the subject can form part of a one year master's or diploma course and lead on to Ph.D. work. The problems which arise are the same wherever the teaching is carried out. The main burden of the teaching at this initial stage of ground clearing must be on the mathematical and statistical techniques used in operational research. In this, there is often an emotional block in the mind of practising operational research scientists. There is a nervousness that in the practical problem-solving field the subject may come to be dominated by the mathematician or the statistician. Consequently some reject completely the need for formal teaching in mathematical statistical methods. They cling to the great romantic view of the classical mixed team, comprising an engineer, a biologist, and a chemist, solving an intricate problem of labour wastage. The need for the knowledge of techniques, however, springs from the realization that, often, when a problem is formulated in a certain way a particular body of techniques will apply and the next stage of the study is considerably accelerated by this recognition. The danger, of course, is that the problem is forced into a particular technical shape, and this was discussed in the chapter on success and failure in operational research. One has to have a balanced view, but it is impossible to be a good practical operational research worker without being a competent theorist. At the very least, the student should have an understanding of probability, distribution theory, hypothesis testing, correlation, time-dependent processes, forecasting and the design of experiments. On the mathematical side the student will need to be competent in mathematical programming, inventory theory, queueing theory, replacement, maintenance and allocation problems.

Linear programming, which is within the general area of mathematical programming, poses an interesting problem. Once one learns to formulate linear problems in linear-programming terms there is, apart from small-scale examples, which are rare, the obvious solution of going on to a computer. In practice this is what is done. Once the problem is formulated in a certain way it is computed and a standard answer emerges. The difficult question to answer is the extent to which a student will need to be taught the basic theoretical algebra used in linear programming, which he might never use in practice, but which he would need to understand if he were to carry out mathematical research in the area. This mathematical knowledge would also be necessary if the student were to try to increase the efficiency with which computers deal with linear-programming problems. It is necessary to indicate to the student at this stage of his development the mechanics of the mathematics involved but it is probably not necessary for him to have a deep detailed knowledge of the separate subjects of the algebra.

But more than an understanding of mathematical and statistical techniques is necessary to provide technical competence in the subject. The student will need to place operational research within the general fabric of science. Hence he will need to have an introduction to the philosophy of science so that he may see how operational research fits into it. But the philosophy of science and in particular the attitude of the operational research worker are not the only valid approaches to problem solving in the practical world. One observes the dismay and confusion of so many scientists who go into industry and government, when they discover that they are faced with problem solvers and decision takers who do not use the scientific method, are not ashamed of not using the scientific method, and are quite successful. Hence it is useful, at the very least, for the student to have an understanding of the underlying philosophical implications of other methods of decision making and of problem solving.

There are also other technical areas which impinge on management. Clearly economics is one such and the student will need an introduction to the basic principles of economics so that he may be aware of those situations in his research when it would be prudent to go to an economist for advice. He will need some knowledge of accounting. So much of the data with which he will be presented will have a spurious accuracy and boldness associated with it which may disappear when he asks the relevant questions applicable to the source of these data.

Management is about people and the social scientist has significant things to say. The young trainee operational research worker, therefore, will need an acquaintance with what the social scientist can do. The industrial engineer is working in the field of the interaction between man and machine. This may well affect production studies which the operational research worker may be called on to carry out and hence he will have to know something of the approach of the industrial engineer.

The purpose of all these studies is not to enable the operational research student to become competent in these other contiguous areas. It would be foolish and impertinent to try to do this in a short lecture course. The purpose is rather to make the operational research worker aware of some of the skills which these other people can bring, and of their basic approach so that he may ask them the right questions and remember to go to them with these right questions.

But central to the craft of operational research is the craft of model building itself. It is in teaching the elements of model building that we still need to learn most. We need to be able to fabricate experimental situations around which the student can formulate his models. The basic drawback of most of the literature on operational research is that it presents a model for each situation and somehow implies that this is the unique model. This is not so. There is something subjective and personal in model building and we need to show the student the way in which different approaches and assumptions about a real situation can lead to different forms of model being produced. Perhaps the greatest shortcoming which operational research faces is this lack of comparative operational research. In any other science the sceptic can be challenged by the experimenter and by the reproduction of the conditions of the experiment he can see for himself the result that will be obtained. This is not so for the operational researcher. First he cannot, at the conclusion of a study, put back the clock and invite the sceptic to carry out his own study. Secondly, even if separate teams carried out research simultaneously along different approaches, they would affect each other and affect the real situation they were studying. Hence comparisons would not be valid. It is difficult to see how one can surmount this particular problem. It is probably going to be one which operational research will live with as long as the subject exists. It is, however, necessary, and this we have failed to do so far, to allow the student to realize that there is nothing particularly virtuous or final about a particular model created in a particular set of circumstances.

Given this basic theoretical approach together with the framework lectures and courses, we will have produced a course for the student which is necessary for his basic competence in the subject but by no means sufficient. The subject has to be placed within a practical problem-solving framework.

The essential feature of all education must be to allow the student to understand how to use the technical skills which have been imparted to him. If one wants to produce a historian, for example, one does this not only by teaching the student a lot of facts about history but also by presenting the student with original documents for him to write his own history. He will do this in the first place by working under the guidance of a competent professional historian. The same thing occurs in the practical sciences. It is not difficult to teach students the facts about electrical engineering. But if one wants to produce students who are going to be able to direct a development programme for an industrial company involving millions of pounds, without bankrupting the company, then one must, at a stage in the training of the student, allow him to work under the guidance of a competent professional engineer and use the principles of design and development in practice. It must be confessed that most British universities, in contrast to American universities, are thoroughly incompetent in this aspect of the educational process. This is because our universities have stemmed from the fine Oxbridge tradition of lack of involvement with the world outside and a failure to realize that they have a fundamentally essential obligation, to form part of the fabric of the community in which they are placed. American universities have historically, from the beginning of the land grant colleges, or cow colleges as they were affectionately called by those British universities who thought themselves somehow superior, always been conscious of the need to serve the local community and in particular the local business and industrial community. Secondly, much of applied research and the development carried out in the United States includes highly significant projects, such as the complete construction of a system for sending an orbiting rocket around Mars, which are developed quite naturally within the academic environment. It is difficult to envisage any British university's being entrusted with such a major national development. Until we do so it is going to continue to be difficult, if not impossible, to teach scientists and technologists anything more than basic tools. The use of the tools has also to be learnt and taught and it is this which our universities are at present failing to do.

Operational research is fortunate in that it is impossible to carry out O.R. within the walls of a university and O.R.

departments are forced, of necessity, to go into the world outside and obtain problems for their students to tackle. There is in this a fearful temptation laid at the door of the universities to throw their students unsupervised into local industry so that they might, as part of their postgraduate training, work on O.R. problems. It is difficult to think of a more stupid method of teaching people to swim than by throwing them in at the deep end and yet this temptation is occasionally yielded to by universities. The student must work as part of a staff–student team so that, under the guidance of a competent professional O.R. worker, he may learn to use the basic tools and techniques with which the lectures referred to above have given him an acquaintance. What sort of projects should these students work on? There is a basic division here about which the author is undecided. On the one hand, one can provide project work in the department which is carried out by members of staff and into which students come from time to time in order to be taught specific parts of the O.R. method. On the other hand one can allocate a student to a single project on which he will work as part of the team throughout his postgraduate training. It is difficult at present to see which of these is better but we can be quite clear about five criteria which these projects must satisfy.

First, they must be significant to the organization which wants them carried out. There is a danger that organizations may wish to support an academic O.R. department and will offer it paid project work as a matter of charity. The academic team will then find themselves doing projects which the company knows are unimportant and this is the worst possible introduction for the student into the potential of the O.R. method.

Secondly, the organization concerned must, unless it has its own captive O.R. group, be prepared to nominate at least one mature member of its staff to work with the academic team on a full-time basis. The team can then carry out a real educational task with the object that when the investigation ends and the team leaves the organization there will be at least one person there who will have worked on an O.R. project and will have seen at first hand why it is that O.R. workers do what they do and how they do it.

The third criterion which the organization must satisfy is that they must be prepared to pay for the study. This is to give the academic team a chance of working under commercial pressure. O.R. is a science which is problem solving within a time scale and, as the chapter on Success and Failure in O.R. points out, it is necessary to report on time in a meaningful fashion. This discipline is imposed on client and university alike.

There are two other criteria which projects have to satisfy. First, they must be meaningful to the academic department— this means that the department must have sufficient work being suggested to it to have the self-confidence to select those projects which, in addition to satisfying the above criteria, will also provide meaningful creative work, not only for the student but also for the professional staff. Obviously, some projects are better at providing fundamental research while others are better at being vehicles for teaching purposes. But for effective work in an O.R. Department, the projects must play their part in one or other of these two roles.

The final criterion which a project must satisfy is at first sight curious. It is that unless there is a significant chance that a project will fail, the O.R. Department should not accept the project into its portfolio. If the team knows how to solve the problem before it even starts work on it then it forms no part of a university department's activity. There must always be the challenge of the unknown. In this, an academic team is no different from a captive industrial team or indeed a commercial consulting team. Unless all O.R. groups are being continually posed problems which at the moment of their posing are unsolvable, then the teams will move into O.R. analysis.

It can be seen, therefore, that an academic O.R. department provides a challenging and exciting life for staff and student alike. It undoubtedly is a tough life. The pleasant routine time-tabling of lectures interspersed by leave and contemplation which forms a part of the ordinary university department has no part here. This is because the demands of project and work are such that it is dangerous to try to separate project work by the calendar. If six continuous months are devoted to teaching techniques and another six continuous to their use, this implants in the mind of the student the idea that technique and practice are separate and distinct. Probably the most important thing of all in operational research is get an intimate interplay between basic tools and basic practice.

We have mentioned above the general need for universities to take an interest in the world outside their own departments. Perhaps operational research, by acting as a bridge not only between different areas of technique but also between the university and the industrial and governmental world, will encourage efforts to approach other departments in the university for specific assistance. It will be good to see an industrial firm going on contract to a university for its basic research and development to be carried out. Universities at present tend to operate so as to maximize their income from the government. This is entirely understandable and within the confines of the strait-jacket of the University Grants Committee there will be a continuing and growing interest in universities in undergraduate teaching because the number of its undergraduate students determines the extent of its financial support from the government. If universities, industry and government departments together fail to realize the great potential of the university for being of use to industry then the university will fail to produce the sort of people who are necessary to support the great growth of technology and science through which we are now passing.

XI

SYNTHESIS

THE purpose of this chapter is to draw together the material of the earlier parts of this book and to try to present a coherent fabric. In doing so we shall try to indicate some of the areas into which the subject might develop and the special responsibilities of those in government and industry whom the operational research scientist is seeking to assist.

At the core of the operational research method lie the model and the objective function, for the attitude of mind of the operational research scientist is specifically revealed in his approach to decision-making problems as an exercise in model construction.

The model is the orderly quantitative construction within which the scientist can experiment, for experimentation is the natural approach of the scientist. This model represents—

1. Those aspects of the "real" situation which are relevant to the decision maker.
2. The logical dependence of these aspects on each other and their joint interaction in producing alternative results.
3. The quantitative values which express the degree of these relationships and their quantitative effect on the results.

It can be seen from the first of these that there is a subjective basis to model building, for the perception of what is real will be personal. Even if our perceptions of reality were all identical, the models constructed would all be different as there is no uniquely correct model. In addition the decision of what aspects are relevant to the decision maker is not clear cut. One man's relevancy is another man's irrelevancy. Hence the model is as personal to the scientist as a putter is to a golfer.

As has been shown, one of the problems we face in O.R. is the difficulty of making comparative or checking studies. The laboratory scientist can always have his work checked by having the experiment repeated. In O.R. this is not possible, for the fact that the research has been carried out at all will have affected the organization, and any repeat studies will be carried out in conditions different from the original ones.

In the more mathematically oriented studies the model may resolve itself into a series of equations or inequalities. Chapter V, which contained an example of the optimum product mix, contained a model which was a set of equations and inequalities, each one of which was a translation from an English language description of some relevant aspect of the "real" problem. This set of mathematical statements is taken by the model builder to contain all that is relevant. In this example it may be clear that the model is comprehensive and exhaustive, although it must be confessed that often, when the conclusions of such a model are presented to the decision maker, he will reject the proffered solution because it offends some qualitative restriction not previously imposed.

Sometimes the construction of the model may involve a series of guesses as to the underlying structure of cause and effect. This is most likely to occur in the underdeveloped areas of O.R., that is social and marketing problems, research and development and government problems (whether local or national). In these situations an important point arises, namely, that proper and extensive experimentation with the model should be carried out so that its correspondence with historical experience may be carefully checked. We have to be very careful not to construct a network of cause and effect that reflects what we wish would happen in a nice tidy world, rather than one which demonstrates how messy reality can be.

So far we have not mentioned the objective function, the existence of which underpins the purpose of the model. In an orderly world we would start with an objective function, in its usual form: $E = f(x_1, x_2, \ldots x_n; y_1, y_2, \ldots y_m)$ and then—

   1. Build the model, expressing the relationships between the x's and the y's.

   2. Forecast the y's.

   3. Select the x's to optimize E.

What generally happens, however, is that the thing the decision taker should be striving for, that is E, is not the starting point of the model-building exercise. We have previously referred to the difficulty of deriving the objectives. Even when there is a single quantifiable objective, its exact form, and hence the units in which E should be expressed, may only emerge during the process of model building. In this very common situation the O.R. worker is like an architect who is asked to design a house, without being given any information about the number of rooms, the total floor area or the total cost. He starts with an assumption of the likely form of the objective function and gradually amends it as the model construction proceeds.

We have specifically gone over this difference between the model and the objective function because there is some confusion, even amongst professional O.R. workers, about the difference between them. But they are, as can be seen, quite distinct and their distinction has to be recognized if we are to appreciate the underlying principles of model building. Their distinction, however, does not imply their independence. They are closely dependent, and indeed sometimes the same model can be used to optimize a number of objective functions.

The major difficulty that arises is that of trying to combine more than one objective into a single scalar quantity. For example, in deciding the comparative merits of different road schemes we may be able to resolve—

   (a) the relative costs of constructing each road;
   (b) the effect each road will have on saving journey time;
   (c) the equivalent cost benefits of these time savings;
   (d) the change in the rate of accidents that each road may
be expected to produce.

Apart from the first, these estimates may well be extremely time-consuming to produce, but they will have to be produced if the road selection is to be based on more than government pressure or horse trading. But even when this is done, how do we equate time, cost and life—the three elements present? Some proposals have been made for this kind of comparison but they do not really resolve the difficulty. And yet, someone is doing this sort of comparison all the time. (Anyone who has pressed the Ministry of Transport for a zebra crossing on a piece of road gets the impression that a minimum number of deaths is demanded before a crossing will be sanctioned.)

In another field, there is the difficulty of comparing even within the same category. Two examples come to mind. In planning a hospital, how do we differentiate the need of patients in various categories of illness? How does a severe hernia compare with a mild thrombosis? An analysis of past decisions could show the relative importance which has been placed on these by those who have been responsible for spending the money. In admitting to a hospital, how do we even decide between patients in the same category of illness, who have suffered it at different intensities for different periods of time?

The second example is in crime detection. How do we judge the efficiency of a detective? If it is by the number of cases he solves, then he may concentrate on the quick and easy cases. If not, we have to be able to rank different sorts of crime. How is this done? Many possibilities exist. They could be ranked by their social cost. They could be ranked by what the police regard as their relative seriousness. This ranking will not correspond with what the members of the public think; nor will any of the foregoing necessarily correspond with what criminologist or penologists assess as the crimes for which detection and punishment will have the greatest deterrence for the future.

It is, perhaps, in the resolution of the multiple objective that operational research faces its greatest challenge. At present we have to content ourselves, in many studies, with evaluating separate objective functions for each class of measurement and leaving it to the decision maker himself to make the final transformation (by subjective processes) on to a common scale.

The place of techniques in operational research should now be clear. The basic skill is in the creation of the model and in testing its significance.

The types of course which need to be developed for a full understanding of the subject and a basis for competence in the subject were outlined in Chapter X. As can be seen the task of the statistical methods is to test the significance of various hypotheses which may be created regarding the structure of the cause and effect relationships. These structures are erected on the basis of a deep and proper understanding of the real situation and this understanding cannot be gained in a hurry. The operational research scientist and the man he is advising must both be patient.

When a structure for the model which is not contradicted by quantitative data collected from the "real" situation has been evolved, the next task is to decide the selection of the controllable variables in the model which will lead to an optimum choice of course of action. As has been explained in previous chapters of this book, sometimes this selection is by mathematical methods, and at others it is made as a result of experimentation. These experimental methods grouped together under the broad heading of "simulation" are ways of evaluating an objective function within the confines of the model. It is not often that statistical methods as such are used to evaluate an objective function. Where they might be thought to be of value, such as in queueing problems, it is often found that the power of the mathematics, or rather the power of the mathematician, is insufficient to grapple with the complex system of equations which is deduced. Hence, as a very broad generalization, one might classify model building as being a phase of the study in which statistical methods are used in order to confirm the significance of a hypothesis, and the methods of mathematics or of simulation are used in attacking the objective function in order to deduce an optimum course of action.

All this assumes that it is possible to state, in a clear form, a pattern of the cause and effect which together are underlying the problems facing the decision maker. It is in such situations that O.R. has so far made its greatest advances. This is not surprising. For once one has a formalized model, it is possible to develop forms of mathematics which are capable of handling a model of this particular nature. In many of these circumstances the greatest brake on progress is the power of a computer to deal with models of these large sizes. Reference has been made in the text to those large-scale models where the basic problem facing the operational research worker is a problem in the area of mathematics, namely the problem on the one hand of creating methods of approach which will enable large-scale models to be broken down into a series of smaller-scale ones and on the other hand, of developing computers so that they are able to take larger-scale models.

But one must not leave the impression that it is only in these large-scale deterministic problems that operational research has its greatest effect. It is tempting to assume that the power of the operational research scientist is in direct proportion to the rigour of the mathematics he is able to deploy. Almost always this is not so. It is generally found that, in those situations where one is applying operational research approaches to problems in which the decision maker has had full information, has had rapid feedback on the extent to which he is achieving his objective and, finally, knows what this objective is, it is difficult for the operational research scientist to gain more than two to five per cent in extra efficiency. The most promising area of operational research lies rather in those fields in which we are groping for the outline of the model. These fields are mainly dominated by problems which arise in the area of social sciences, marketing, and research and development.

A previous chapter, which was devoted to a study of the use of operational research in some fields of human problems, outlined some of the approaches which have been made to this very difficult problem. One of the best compendiums showing the interaction between operational research and the social sciences is *O.R. and the Social Sciences*.[1] This exhaustive volume covers the field of organization and control, social effects of policies and their measurement, conflict resolution and control, and the systems concept as a frame of reference. This conference showed in a very interesting way the inter-relationship between the operational research worker and the social scientist. It showed the great difficulty which the

[1] Edited by J. R. LAWRENCE (Wiley, 1966).

former faces in these areas in trying to derive measures for the performance of social systems which are relevant to their objectives. To derive these measures it is going to be necessary to have a firm understanding of, in very crude terms, the input to a social system and its output. Not only do we need a way of relating the desirability of alternative outputs but we must also have some way of ranking the objectives, for it is a basic feature of social systems that input, output, and objectives all contain within them numbers of factors which arise on different scales of measurement.

It is interesting to reflect why operational research workers have been so slow and so reluctant to enter into this social field. We are, after all, dealing with systems in which the basic concepts are man, machines, money, materials and markets. It is rare indeed that any system with which we deal has not got man included in it and yet we have constantly ignored man as a factor. The basic reason why the operational research scientist has been so reluctant to enter into this field is because we nearly all come from the field of the natural sciences. We are conditioned to measurement, the more precise the better. We are brought up in systems which are largely physical and in which we can see the pattern of cause and effect. The first developments of operational research in industry and government have been in dealing with physical systems. The original operational research studies before and during the Second World War were studies of the use of man in physical systems such as depth charges, convoys, radar and so on. The first introduction of operational research into industry was in the study of production systems. It has been natural that operational research should move into these physical settings. As has already been seen the main development of operational research away from the purely physical system has been into marketing, which is a half-way house between the physical and the social. Areas such as the social sciences are so un-physical to the operational research worker as to appear almost metaphysical. And yet we cannot claim to be develop-ing our studies properly until, together with the social scientist, we derive measures of performance and of attain-ment. The danger which faces the operational research scientist in these fields is exactly that which faces him in every other field, namely that he will be led to produce models which describe what he would like the world to be rather than what it really is. For example, he may be led to derive models which enable certain types of algebra to be deployed with great effectiveness. These types of algebra can be very effective provided one has the correct model. The use of techniques in this area is very much like the use of ladders in the game of snakes and ladders. If one can get the starting conditions right then one can use a technique ladder to move very rapidly through the game. The problem is that one may so force the starting conditions in order to use the technique ladder that an unrealistic problem is solved. Some of the papers which have been written by operational re-search workers in the social field suffer in this respect. The other danger which may arise is that of producing measures which satisfy decisions already taken. In some uses of cost benefit analysis, for example, one is sometimes uneasily aware that the costs of the time people spend in travelling, for example, have been rigged so as to produce a certain con-clusion leading to a certain course of action. Often, in the social field, if we evaluate the revenue output against the cost input, as in the construction of a roadway, nothing would ever get built for the cost return would be insufficient. In these situations the danger, as has been said, is that we shall produce measures for the residual effects which enable some-thing which is thought intuitively to be socially desirable, to be shown also to be analytically respectable.

These problems arise in their greatest complexity in the area of research and development. One of the most pressing problems which faces both the government and the individual company is the amount of money which should be invested each year in basic research, applied research, and development. A second problem is the control of ongoing research projects, and finally there is the problem of assessing both the probability of a particular piece of research's succeeding within a given length of time and the dividends, whether national or to the company, stemming from this success.

Some approaches have, of course, already been made. It is possible to look at the total research budget for an organization in the light of seeing or forecasting what would happen to the total profitability of the company if no further research or development were undertaken. As existing products die out and lose their market there would be a run-down in the total income to the company with a corresponding run-down in profits. It is sometimes possible to take historical research expenditure and to see the level at which this should be maintained in order to have an adequate replenishment of products in the company's total range. Clearly, and this is confirmed by experience, the amount of research needed, therefore, is related to the length of life of a typical product which the company is offering. The percentage of total turnover which different industries will spend on research and development is highly correlated with the rate of replenishment of products which they are offering in the market.

The control of ongoing research is a very difficult subject. Some attempts have been made by means of the methods of critical path which were examined in an earlier chapter, to forecast the demands to be made on a research organization in terms of the researches currently under way. It is not very common for a research department to survey critically its existing commitments and to forecast the demands on men, money and equipment which if they continue, they are going to generate in the future. These critical path studies have shown up some bottlenecks in one or other of these three basic factors. Other studies, particularly in the drug industry, have been devoted to showing the effect of different numbers of people of different characteristics being deployed on a particular research project. A way of bringing together all these approaches is, of course, simulation. It is possible to structure the future progress of a piece of research along the line of a decision tree. A decision tree is a way of surveying ahead the branching decision points in an ongoing project and of forecasting all of what is likely to happen if each of these branches are taken.

In such a decision tree approach, which is not uncommon in a financial analysis, it is possible to look ahead and see along which line research projects should be allowed to proceed. This enables the resources to be concentrated at any time on those particular parts of the research which are likely to lead to a maximum pay-off. The pay-off is in terms of the sort of product which is likely to emerge if the research goes along that particular branch of the tree.

This leads one into considering the productivity of research scientists as such. So far measures of productivity have been evolved including the number of patents issued, the total capital spending on technology (which may be assumed to follow, say three years, after successful research is completed) the total number of papers published in the literature and so on. Unfortunately, most of the measures of productivity which have been derived seem to show a falling off in productivity among scientists over the past twenty years. (This is probably a reflection of the poverty of the indices which have been derived rather than of the productivity of the scientists themselves. However, this is only a conjecture and it would be interesting to see development of studies in this area.) Further studies have been carried out to show the effect of the literature on scientists. Some investigations have shown the markedly greater cheapness of distributing literature in the form of abstracts rather than in the form of full published papers. The costs per reader page of some of the papers appearing in some of the main journals in chemistry, for example, are quite astronomical and tests which have been carried out on the comprehensibility of much shortened papers compared with full length ones have shown that there would not be much loss in presenting much shorter papers in the literature. All this assumes that the purpose of a paper is to extend knowledge and not to advance the prestige of the author.

From time to time reference has been made to the problem of introducing operational research at government level. It is a curious reflection that whereas the first operational research studies arose within the government on military problems, they have not until very recently begun to penetrate civil government. There are some studies currently under way in the Home Office and in the Ministry of Technology and in addition other work has been carried out by the Royal Institute of Public Administration in local government. But compared with the total size of the problems involved the forces which have been deployed have been quite derisory. Those who have been concerned with decision making at government level must be frightened at the lack of relevant quantitative data available to underpin these decisions. Even the nationally trumpeted figures for imports and exports are subject to such gross errors as to be quite a meaningless monthly exercise. There is a need for a thorough refurnishing of government statistical services, which have been allowed to lapse far behind their requirements as an aid to proper decision making. The greatest need, of course, is for the employment of operational research scientists within the government system. It is encouraging that at the present time some moves in this direction are being made. Much, however, remains to be done and that so much does remain to be done is perhaps the responsibility of the operational research scientist himself. This leads on to the final point.

It is unfortunate that over the last twenty years operational research has had a certain huckster element associated with it. It has been over-sold. It has been presented as an infallible poultice to be slapped on every decision maker's boil. It is, of course, a research activity and as such is acquainted with failure. So many people (including the present author) have spent so much time encouraging industry and government to develop and use operational research that we have now succeeded in stimulating a demand for operational research scientists which it is not possible to supply. The danger is that this demand will be met by the use of scientists who are incompetent in the subject. This will lead to a higher failure rate and the subject is still small enough to suffer when there are failures in it. We need first of all to step up the flow of well trained recruits into the subject. We need secondly to retain in the subject the experienced and senior operational research workers who might be tempted to move into management or into other fields. We need to encourage industry and government to be both patient and helpful. We need them to be patient since the subject is still new and faced with a number of areas where it is groping for understanding. We need, however, perhaps most of all, a different approach from management to decision-making problems. Perhaps the greatest problem which the operational research worker faces is in the type of manager with whom he deals, the manager who cannot think conceptually in structural form about the decisions with which he is faced. We need in fact a thorough overhaul of management training. The first steps which are being taken are, of course, encouraging but so much more needs to be done. It is probably true that in every study which the operational research worker undertakes it is shown that the great improvement in efficiency and in profits which can stem from these studies will be achieved far more by better management than by harder work from the labour force. We have concentrated so much in this country on trying to sweat more out of the worker that we have neglected to concentrate on the rank inefficiencies in so much of business and government.

We hope we have shown what this subject is about. It is the attempt of the natural scientist to create models of the consequences of decisions in complex management situations. The successful resolution of these models depends on the understanding the operational research worker has of the natural processes underpinning the decision, on his competence in creating models which adequately reflect these complex situations, on his understanding of what the objectives in the situation are, or ought to be, and on the ability of management to diagnose their problems in such a way that the operational research worker is brought in as one of the specialists who have something relevant to say. The manager should not only be sufficiently forceful to encourage the actual application of the results but, most important of all, he should himself realize that he has a problem. Perhaps the most important advice to management and government alike is to realize that they have a problem.

SELECT BIBLIOGRAPHY

REFERENCE has already been made at the appropriate places in this book to works which will amplify points which have had to be made very briefly. The purpose of this short section is to give an outline of further reading in the subject for those who might be interested. The background mathematical methods are written up in many works. The simplest and shortest account of some of these mathematical and statistical techniques is given in *Operational Research*, by MAKOWER and WILLIAMSON (E.U.P., 1967). Another similar book which covers a slightly wider field is *Management and Mathematics*, by FLETCHER and CLARKE published by Business Publications, 1964. Finally for those who may wish to indulge in more extensive mathematics there is an admirable book, *Operational Research—Methods and Problems*, by SASIENI, YASPAN and FRIEDMAN (Wiley, 1959).

Reference has been made in this book to a number of special areas of the subject and a number of contiguous specialties which have influenced the development of Operational Research. An area of significant current interest is that of the behavioural sciences and there are four books which could be consulted with profit. They are *Operational Research and the Social Sciences*, edited by LAWRENCE (Tavistock, 1966), *New Perspectives in Organization Research*, by COOPER, LEAVITT and SHELLY (Wiley, 1964) and *A Behavioural Theory of the Firm*, by CYERT and MARCH (Prentice-Hall, 1964). The best understanding of Operational Research is gained through case study material. This will be found in the volumes which cover the proceedings of the international conferences on Operational Research, which are published every three years. There have so far been four such publications, of consistently increasing length, and these are issued by English Universities Press. Other very useful case studies, combined with an excellent account of the development of mathematical theories underlying simulation, are given in *The Art of Simulation*, by TOCHER

(E.U.P., 1964). There are, finally, a few books which present, in a coherent fabric, the background of the Operational Research method and some of its philosophy. The shortest of these accounts is *The Manager's Guide to Operational Research*, by RIVETT and ACKOFF (Wiley, 1963). An introduction to the fabric of the subject springing very largely from a rigorous examination of the scientific method is given in *Scientific Method*, by ACKOFF (Wiley, 1963). Another comprehensive survey of the philosophical basis of Operational Research and the way it fits into the management sciences is given in *Decision and Control*, by BEER (Wiley, 1966).

Clearly, this reading list is not comprehensive. It is, however, suggested as a first list to those who want to take their reading further. These books all contain numerous references for further study and hence can be regarded as an entry point to the study of the use of science in aiding management decision making.

INDEX